Emerging Class in Papua New Guinea
The Telling of Difference

This accessible and pioneering study of social class in contemporary Papua New Guinea deals with the new elite, its culture and institutions, and its relationship to the broader society. The Papua New Guinea described here is not a place of exotic tribesmen, but a modernizing society, shaped by global forces and increasingly divided on class lines. Focusing on Wewak, a typical commercial centre, the authors describe the lifestyle of those elite who frequent its golf clubs and Rotary gatherings. In so doing, they bring home the ways in which differences of status are created, experienced and justified. In a country with a long tradition of egalitarianism, it has become at once possible and plausible for relatively affluent "nationals" to present themselves in a wide range of contexts as fundamentally superior to "bushy" people, to blame the poor for their misfortunes and to turn their backs on their less successful neighbors and relatives.

DEBORAH B. GEWERTZ is G. Henry Whitcomb Professor of Anthropology at Amherst College, Massachusetts and FREDERICK K. ERRINGTON is Charles A. Dana Professor of Anthropology at Trinity College, Connecticut. They are joint authors of three previous books on Papua New Guinea, *Cultural Alternatives and a Feminist Anthropology* (1987), and *Twisted Histories, Altered Contexts* (1991), both published by Cambridge University Press, and *Articulating Change in the Last "Unknown"* (1995). Professor Gewertz's other publications include *Sepik River Societies* (1988), and *Myths of Matriarchy Reconsidered* (1988), and numerous articles. Professor Errington's other publications include *Karavar* (1974), *Manners and Meaning in West Sumatra* (1984), and numerous articles. They are currently engaged in a joint project about changing foodways in Papua New Guinea.

Emerging Class in Papua New Guinea: The Telling of Difference

Deborah B. Gewertz Frederick K. Errington

CAMBRIDGE
UNIVERSITY PRESS

PUBLISHED BY THE PRESS SYNDICATE OF THE UNIVERSITY OF CAMBRIDGE
The Pitt Building, Trumpington Street, Cambridge, United Kingdom

CAMBRIDGE UNIVERSITY PRESS
The Edinburgh Building, Cambridge, CB2 2RU, UK http://www.cup.cam.ac.uk
40 West 20th Street, New York, NY 10011–4211, USA http://www.cup.org
10 Stamford Road, Oakleigh, Melbourne 3166, Australia

First published 1999

Printed in the United Kingdom at the University Press, Cambridge

Typeset in Baskerville 11/12.5 pt [CE]

A catalogue record for this book is available from the British Library

Library of Congress cataloguing in publication data

Gewertz, Deborah B., 1948–
Emerging class in Papua New Guinea: the telling of difference /
Deborah B. Gewertz, Frederick K. Errington.
p. cm.
Includes bibliographical references and index.
ISBN 0 521 65212 X
1. Social classes – Papua New Guinea – Wewak. 2. Wewak (Papua New Guinea) – Social conditions. I. Errington, Frederick Karl.
II. Title.
HN932.W48G48 1999
305.5′09953 – dc21 98–42341 CIP

ISBN 0 521 65212 X hardback
ISBN 0 521 65567 6 paperback

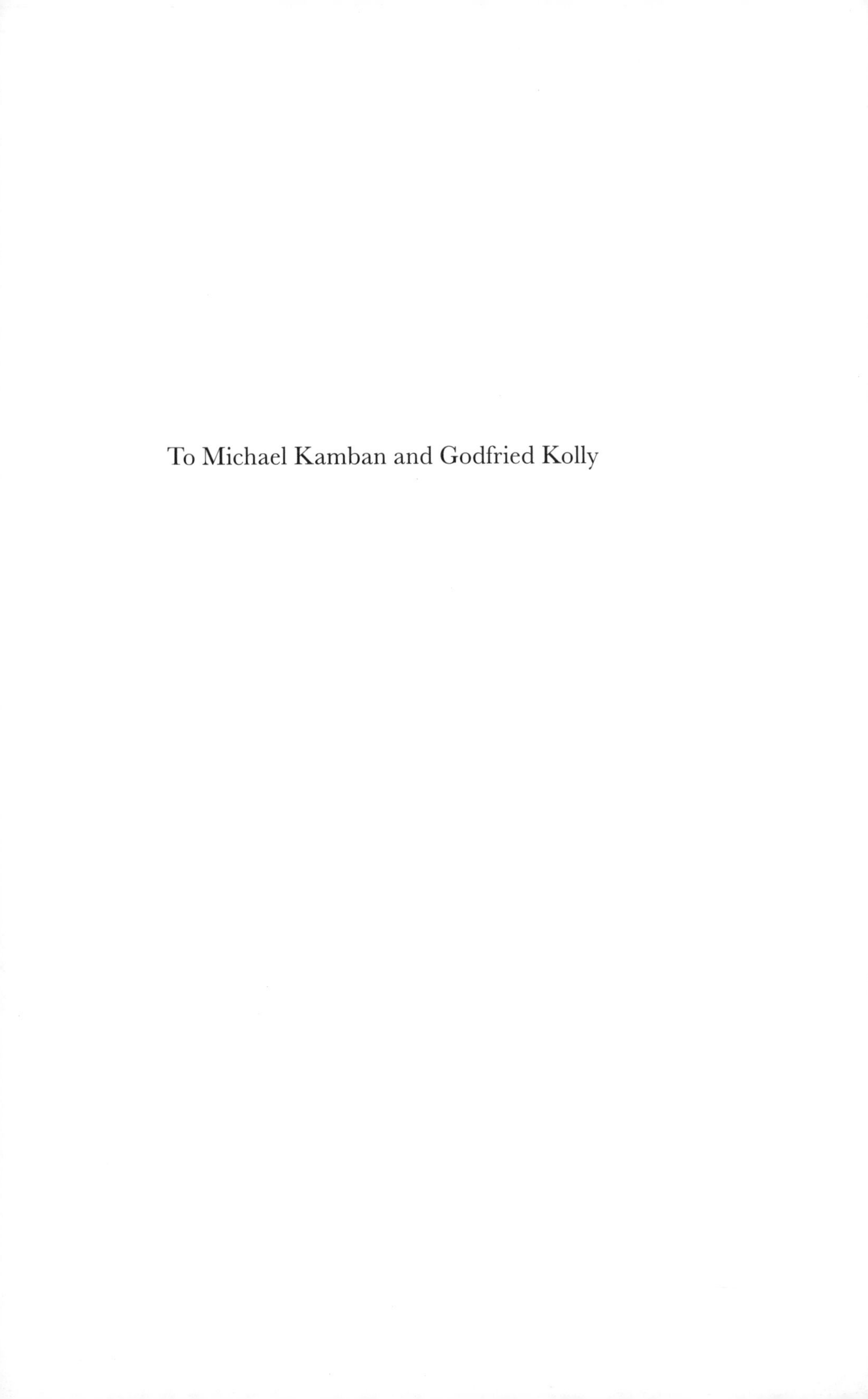

To Michael Kamban and Godfried Kolly

Contents

Illustrations

MAPS

PHOTOGRAPHS

Acknowledgments

Despite the frustrations and perplexities that research and writing invariably provide, we feel most fortunate to have had anthropological lives. We feel fortunate largely because, over the course of these lives (during the seven times we have visited Papua New Guinea and during the times in between), we have conversed, argued, collaborated and shared hospitality with many compelling people – both abroad and at home, both in the field and in the academy. And these various engagements have generally been about issues that, all have thought, matter: issues that have made the talk, the arguments, and the sociability worth having – not to mention, the money it has cost (we trust) worth spending.

Concerning those who have importantly engaged with us on the research and writing of this particular book, we especially thank: Warwick Andrew, John Ballard, Olivier and Theresa Meric de Bellefon, Norrie and Berta Bomai, James Carrier, Elizabeth Cox, Robert Foster, Janet Gyatso, Eunice and Warren Hanson, Margaret Hayward, Antony Hooper, Peter Johnson, Dan Jorgensen, Evangeline Kaina, Michael Kamban, Stuart Kirsch, Bradley Klein, Godfried Kolly, Rena Lederman, Andrew Masal, Laura Martin, Andrew and Roselyn Munap, Eugene Ogan, Phillip Raif, Sampson Saman, Lucy Simogun, Mary Sindrouw, William Standish, Ralf Stuttgen, Karen Sykes, Eileen and Eric Tang, Rose Uri, Tekla and Roderik Vehmeyer, and Benny Wapi. In addition, we thank the many, many friends and acquaintances whose names we simply could not list here, but who generously provided us with time and information during our stay in Wewak. And finally, as always, we specially thank Carolyn Errington for her careful and discerning editing.

Concerning those who paid for it all, we appreciate generous grants from (listed alphabetically): Amherst College, the National Science Foundation, Trinity College and the Wenner-Gren Foundation for Anthropological Research.

Concerning permissions granted, we are grateful to Goodman Fielder International for allowing us to use the Eta margarine ad as our cover illustration (and to Robert Foster for calling our attention to it when he visited us in Papua New Guinea). In addition, we are grateful to the *Journal of the Royal Anthropological Institute* and to the *Contemporary Pacific* for publishing versions of the arguments we develop in chapters 1 and 2.

Concerning our collaboration, we savor its basis in thoroughly commensurate differences.

Introduction: The twists and turns of difference

This book is our telling of the ways that class inequalities in contemporary Papua New Guinea have been convincingly, and with telling effect, told. It is about the contexts and processes, both "traditional" and "modernist,"[1] within which many relatively affluent Papua New Guineans were conveying to whole categories of their countrymen that the latter lacked viable or legitimate claims on significant resources. It is about how it has become both possible and plausible for these relatively affluent "nationals" – even those living in rather modest urban centers like Wewak, the capital of the East Sepik Province and the fifth largest town in a Papua New Guinea of some 4 million people – to present themselves in an apparently diverse range of contexts to other Papua New Guineans (including members of their own cultural groups) as fundamentally superior.[2]

It is about how, by 1996 – scarcely two decades after the formal end of the era in which an Australian child could address a grown "native" man as "boy"[3] – a Papua New Guinean physician could comfortably distinguish himself from others in his cultural group by calling them "bushy" and himself "civilized"; how Papua New Guinean members of Wewak's Rotary Club could remind each other not to invite countrymen of the "wrong" sort to their annual benefit auction; how a group of Papua New Guinean businesswomen could designate themselves as models of entrepreneurial success while implicitly blaming poor women for their own continuing impoverishment; how a Papua New Guinean store owner could snap his fingers at his golf caddies so that they would move with more alacrity; how Papua New Guinean members of Wewak's golf and yacht clubs could congratulate themselves on the exclusivity of their organizations; how a Papua New Guinean politician could advise the rural poor that they should no longer aspire to the ownership of

Toyota Land Cruisers – such as he, in fact, owned – but would have to content themselves with water buffaloes as the appropriate technology for their scaled-back futures; and how a Papua New Guinean national court judge could define the "ordinary" man as the well-educated, urban man.

This is a book, thus, about an "historical phenomenon, [one] unifying a number of disparate and seemingly unconnected events, both in the raw material of experience and in consciousness" (Thompson, 1964: 9). It concerns the contemporary workings in Papua New Guinea of class – not "as a 'structure,' nor even as a 'category,' but as something which in fact happens (and can be shown to have happened) in human relationships" (Thompson, 1964: 9). As suggested by the examples just provided, the relationships which have become class emerged as men and women came to "feel and articulate the identity of their [material] interests as between themselves, and as against other men [and women] whose interests [were] different from (and usually opposed to) theirs" (Thompson, 1964: 9). Class, we show, has been happening in Papua New Guinea, and its happenings have increasingly become evident to many.

This is a book which many Papua New Guineans had hoped could never be written. After the obvious inequities of the colonial caste system had abated, they had hoped the strenuous egalitarianism which had characterized much (though not all) indigenous Papua New Guinean life (at least among men) might be preserved as the valued basis of a new political order.[4] It was an egalitarianism where differences were largely commensurate, based upon fluctuating degree rather than, as with class (to say nothing of caste), upon fixed kind: where powerful men and powerful groups had, for the most part, simply more of what all others had (such as pigs, shells, wives, ritual knowledge, trading partners and allies) rather than sharply differential access to economic and cultural capital (such as employment networks, educational opportunities, and sartorial, gustatory and conversational skills [cf. Goody, 1982; Bourdieu, 1977]).[5] Correspondingly, it was an egalitarianism where, because personal and collective fortunes and alliances often shifted, the powerful rarely remained perpetually so; where perceptions of life's prospects were shaped by the relatively realistic recognition that "big men" and "rubbish men" (and certainly their immediate descendants) could, in the course of events, interchange places on a single continuum.[6]

We, too, had shared the hope that this egalitarianism, one which had in fact first drawn us to Papua New Guinea, could be preserved. However, we soon began to worry that it would prove especially vulnerable to the imposition of those incommensurate differences – those inequalities of kind – existing between "first" and "third" worlds: we feared that such a new postcolonial political order would be fundamentally undermined if Papua New Guineans found themselves depleted of resources and value. Hence, for some time in our writings we had been concerned, for instance, that Papua New Guineans were, for a pittance, yielding up their mineral and timber resources to international corporations and that they were performing their culture as professional primitives – as the "embodiment of the exotic" (Gewertz and Errington, 1991a: 205) – for an international tourist industry. It was, though, only in our most recent work that we have begun to give full attention to perhaps a more insidious (if related) threat. This threat had already attracted the concern of some Papua New Guineans themselves.

It had been in order to define, defend and preserve for a new nation what was best about indigenous forms of egalitarianism that the Papua New Guinean lawyer and now senior politician, Bernard Narakobi, wrote *The Melanesian Way*. In that book, published five years after Independence, he lamented the emergence of a "PNG elite – be they civil servants, politicians, religious officials or private businessmen and women ... [who] have no authentic touch or feeling for rural and urban poor but they seem to know all the answers to the problems of the poor." He pledged that "firm steps" would be taken to preclude a "class society ... emerging in this country" (1980: 108).

What instead happened

As our initial examples suggest, "firm steps" were not, however, taken. That this was so has stemmed from the fact – and from the complex responses of an emerging nation to the fact – that Papua New Guinea was, and has remained, extremely vulnerable to an international economy. Indeed, in 1975, the year of Independence, Papua New Guinea "held the dubious distinction of being the most dependent independent country in the world. Forty-five percent of the government budget came in the form of an Australian grant. On top of this, Papua New Guinea had one of the highest propensities to import of any country" (Turner, 1990: 33). Indeed, virtually everything not produced by the subsistence sector had to be imported and imports rapidly came to be, for both urban workers and many rural smallholders, necessary luxuries: canned fish, rice and kerosene, to say nothing of outboard motors, cars and trucks. Exports, on the other hand, were almost entirely primary products, subject to substantial international price fluctuations. (Initially these were plantation crops; subsequently timber and minerals.) Moreover, during the early years of Independence, it was expatriates (largely Australians) who filled most managerial and technical positions, both in the government and in the private sector. Indeed, "[o]wnership of the formal economy was largely vested in foreign hands. Papua New Guineans owned few businesses, and those they did own were small" (Turner, 1990: 33).

Many Papua New Guinea politicians, contemplating the future status of their postcolonial nation, decried these circumstances of dependence and explored alternatives. In so doing, they commissioned a report from a (largely expatriate) team recruited through the Overseas Development Group of the University of East Anglia. This was, at the time, "the most radical center for development studies in the United Kingdom ... [whose members] adhered to the various socialist strategies carried out, for example, in some African countries such as Tanzania" (Jacobsen, 1995: 232). From such explorations, the vision of national sovereignty that emerged in newly independent Papua New Guinea was centered on greater self-reliance.

To implement this vision, Papua New Guinea began a policy of "localization." Papua New Guineans were steadily to replace expatriates in the public service. (In 1972, there were 7,900 expatriate public servants; in 1988, 1,719 [Turner, 1990: 44].) Such a policy proved convenient, not only ideologically (given socialist leanings) but practically. This was so because the (colonial and postcolonial) educational system, though highly restrictive at its upper levels, was nonetheless producing appreciable numbers of secondary and tertiary graduates who expected good jobs. By localizing the civil service (and in the absence of a strong private sector), the government could assure employment of – in fact, become the principal employer for – the more advanced graduates of its own educational system. The government, however, did more than simply localize, it also expanded in response to political exigencies. It expanded not only by continuing to absorb the educated, but also by providing a new layer of bureaucracy – and politicians – at the provincial level in response to pressures (especially from resource-rich areas) for greater regional control (see Conyers, 1979; Standish, 1979; Filer, 1990). (In 1960, there were about 5,000 employed by the government; in 1990, with a population of less than 4 million, 50,000 were so employed [Millett, 1993: 14].)

At the same time, Papua New Guinea sought to enhance its self-reliance through generating more private sector employment and greater national revenues. (The government could only afford to employ so many; its own expenses were high and the Australian subsidy – while still substantial – was diminishing.) The government, thus, encouraged major foreign enterprises to develop the country's rich natural resources. So as to control the influence of such foreign enterprises and to generate income for its burgeoning public service sector, the government insisted that it be a major stockholder in such facilities as the copper and gold mines at Bougainville, Ok Tedi, Pogera and Lihir, and the oil fields at Kutubu.

To be sure, with this "progressive localisation in both public and private sectors . . . [there were] more Papua New Guineans earning higher salaries" (Turner, 1990: 76). And government revenue from resource extraction was considerable. Yet, Papua New Guinea's economy remained, and has continued to remain, vulnerable, with its principal expenditures still going to imports and its principal income still coming from exports of primary resources (Millett, 1993). The government bureaucracy has become relatively large and expensive, financed mainly by such exports, and the private sector has remained small. (In 1990, the some 50,000 government employees comprised over one-quarter of those [relatively few] wage-employed Papua New Guineans [Millett, 1993: 14, 20].) The major extractive enterprises have remained substantially staffed at the managerial and technical levels by expatriates; and once on line, these enterprises have become sufficiently mechanized so as to provide only limited (at least relative to the government) employment of local people. Moreover, these enterprises were ultimately controlled by multinational corporations whose policies and profits (and payments to the Papua New Guinean government) were subject to the vagaries of a world market.

The general goal of self-reliance also led to such fiscal measures as high import duties and an artificially bolstered kina (the national currency). These policies promised the trappings of a strong economy: taxation of imports would encourage local production and in turn self-sufficiency, and a bolstered kina would remain strong, vigorous and internationally competitive. Actually, the government's fiscal measures did little to foster real economic viability. For instance, the strong kina itself probably has contributed to Papua New Guinea's dependency: an artificially elevated kina has likely discouraged domestic production by creating products too costly for ready sale on the world market.

Not coincidentally (given an established bureaucracy), the high kina did keep the civil servants reasonably happy. Despite tariffs, their salaries accorded them considerable buying power, certainly relative to most other Papua New Guineans. For the majority of citizens, however, the best they could expect under these circumstances was for the government to use a significant portion of its revenues – principally its shareholder portion of profits – to provide basic social and infrastructural public services. But, even these expectations were to prove largely unfulfilled. Because the government was unwilling or unable to provide services efficiently and because income from the resource sector (though considerable) proved less than anticipated, the government eventually faced increasing fiscal difficulties. Contributing to these difficulties was an insurrection on Bougainville, leading to the closure of the major mine there (Filer, 1990). In this situation, the government not only lost mine revenue, but had to pay out a large amount for an ineffectual military effort to suppress the rebellion. Eventually, it literally ran out of the foreign exchange on which its still import-dependent economy rested.[7]

An Australian government report summarized these circumstances: "For Papua New Guinea, 1994 was a year of crises. Despite strong growth in government revenues the budget deficit spiraled . . . There was a loss in confidence by international lenders and the government was forced to float the kina because of the sharp drop in foreign exchange reserves" (AusAid, 1995: 17). The terms of the ensuing bail-out by the World Bank and International Monetary Fund required the government to accept "structural adjustments." These were the provisions (ostensibly) necessary to reduce governmental expenses and to increase productivity and international competitiveness. They included retrenching civil servants and decreasing existing "subsidies" to health and educational facilities; they also recommended the registration and subsequent privatization of traditionally owned land. In these ways, it was argued, governmental costs not only would be reduced but responsibilities for social services would be appropriately shifted from the government to the actual users; moreover, users, encouraged to invest in and borrow on their land, would be better able to pay for services and otherwise sustain themselves.

The 1994 crises were a heightening – and, for many, a clarification – of what had been happening for some time. Most of the relatively few Papua New Guineans with good jobs remained well-positioned, while most of the myriad with no regular income became additionally deprived – not just of what had become essential commodities but of what had become essential services.[8] Regardless of whether the "structural adjustments" imposed by the World Bank and International Monetary Fund could ever prove practically (or morally) justifiable, the new stringency Papua New Guineans were experiencing when we encountered them in 1996 had led to a further sharpening of social distinction.

There was obviously still money around for some. Most of the extractive industries were still running and government spending was still substantial. Indigenous contractors were still getting contracts for, among other things, government and foreign-aid financed projects such as for road maintenance, bridge construction, and land reclamation. Politicians were still using their "slush funds" to travel to Cairns (for entertainment or, perhaps, to invest in Queensland real estate[9]) and to purchase votes or otherwise mollify key constituents. Civil servants were, generally, still receiving salaries. Business and professional people were still selling products and services. Agricultural entrepreneurs were still earning income through the sale of such produce as coffee and betel nut. And craftspeople were still earning (some) money through the sale of their artifacts. But opportunities had become progressively constricted and those who were comfortably through the door – those (as in our book's initial examples) of the relative elite who had substantial access to what money there was – were increasingly differentiated and were increasingly differentiating themselves from others.

This elite – these company managers, politicians, civil servants, professionals and assorted businesspeople and entrepreneurs – were mostly middle class (given that their primarily resource-extractive economy was, largely, controlled by non-Papua New Guineans, by international owners of capital). This is not to say, we must emphasize, that there were no important differences in access to power and resources among those of the middle class. Thus, for example, there were many differences between newly credentialed primary school teachers, whose parents had had little formal education and no salaried employment, and well-educated senior civil servants, whose parents had been advantageously placed during the colonial period. Comparably, there were many differences between small-scale retailers, whose businesses serviced primarily those squatters who lived in their vicinities, and major wholesalers, whose businesses involved direct engagement with overseas producers, distributors and financiers. In addition, there were important differences between local politicians, whose election to the Provincial Assembly gave them only limited power and resources, and national politicians, whose election to the Parliament gave them access to an extensive public trough and to influence peddling. Nor – as these examples imply – is it to say that there were no individuals whose class positions were ambiguous or in transition. (Rural schoolteachers, although salaried, may have had more in common, for instance, with subsistence-oriented villagers than with affluent urban dwellers.) Nor, finally, is it to say that there were no differences in interests within this middle class. Certainly the proposed structural adjustments would unequally affect civil servants subject to retrenchment and agricultural entrepreneurs anxious to buy and sell land (Thompson and MacWilliam, 1992).

But it is to say that many middle-class Papua New Guineans were increasingly, and with crucial consequences, becoming less and less connected to the poor and their problems. Indeed, those of the middle class – especially its more affluent members – were both engaged and caught up in the social and cultural work of creating new forms of distinction. Through this work a crucial shift in daily life was being rendered normal and reasonable. The consequence was that many of those once contenders in the same, relatively fluid, political field could become regarded – could become redefined – as ontologically inferior.

theory of existence

Why study class happenings in Papua New Guinea?

In its focus on the social and cultural work of creating new forms of distinction, this book is both about Papua New Guinea and about much of the rest of the contemporary world.[10] Thus, to bring it back home, this book is at least indirectly about the students we have taught – and not just those attending elite private colleges – who have accepted (often, we suspect, without experiencing the slightest dark night of the soul) their successes as having had little to do with their frequently privileged social contexts (of good neighborhoods, decent secondary schools, and special tutoring). Rather, they have tended to attribute their achievements to their own cleverness as well as to having made the right choices.[11] And, correspondingly, they have believed that those unable similarly to prevail have (largely) themselves to blame. By showing how the instantiation and internalization of class-based inequalities have proceeded in Papua New Guinea, we mean to convince our students (and others) that they, also, have been subject to – and in most cases beneficiaries of – comparable processes.

While such a telling of the happenings of class could be grounded in a variety of ethnographic contexts, we think Papua New Guinea a particularly apposite case. By focusing on Papua New Guinea circumstances, we can show with special clarity not only that these processes have taken hold, but also how this shift in the nature and understanding of relationships has been propounded in increasingly insistent and compelling fashions. This is because the social forces in Papua New Guinea that were (among other things) establishing and maintaining class-based inequalities were more than affecting lives: they were rapidly transforming lives. Many Papua New Guineans were explicit in their recognition of these ongoing transformations. For example, we were often told by one or another informant that his father lived in the "Stone Age," while his own son lived in the "Space Age."[12] Although we would contest the evolutionism inherent in many such appraisals, there is no doubt that change in Papua New Guinea has been experienced as precipitous.

For most Papua New Guineans (even for those having the longest colonial histories), significant encounters with the European presence were likely to have first occurred since the late nineteenth century. The Europeans initiated changes that were sometimes dramatic, frequently intense, and often indelible. That these changes occurred within a relatively brief and recent time has meant that they could be remembered and locally discussed with considerable clarity. (In areas where "first contact" was more recent, the inception of these changes could be documented by eye-witnesses.) Therefore, Papua New Guineans, whose readily available experiences might have encompassed the pre-contact and the transnational and whose sensibilities might have encompassed the indigenous and the post-modern, were not only caught up in dramatic change but were also often preoccupied in thinking about and negotiating that change. Hence, Papua New Guinea's relatively recent and compressed colonial history, conjoined with its frequently egalitarian indigenous ethos, has made it a particularly informative context for considering transformative processes – especially those of class happenings.

Because we began our field research in Papua New Guinea prior to its Independence, we too have been involved in, and have been able to write about, many of these changes and transformations. Certainly, it has been our conversations, sustained over time, with Papua New Guinean friends and acquaintances about their varying pasts, presents and prospects that have helped us in writing this book – the latest in what we have come to think of as a serial ethnography. The local knowledge we have garnered from years of work among the Chambri of Papua New Guinea's East Sepik Province, both in their relatively remote home fishing villages and in their urban, squatter settlement in Wewak,[13] has been essential to our present focus on the unfolding processes of distinction. Especially, insight into the lives of the rural and urban poor, known as the "grass roots" (and our consequent distress at the distress of our friends among them), has been central to understanding (and working to convey) these processes. Class happenings, after all, are class *relationships*, wherein (for example) a middle class comes into existence only in association with a lower class (see Ossowski, 1963; Thompson, 1964). One cannot, thus, describe middle-class sociality and culture without discussing the creation and experience of new forms of invidious distinctions affecting privileged and deprivileged alike. The lives of those Papua New Guineans who have benefited from key socioeconomic changes cannot be separated from the lives of those who have not benefited.

By conveying these increasingly divergent lives we will, in essence, be demonstrating the effects of not taking the "firm steps" that Narakobi called for: the growing significance of the happenings of class to the organization, experience and direction of late twentieth-century life in Papua New Guinea.

What is Melanesian about Papua New Guinean class happenings?

We have argued that Papua New Guinea could be a generally informative context concerning (to repeat) the ways that men and women have come to "feel and articulate the identity of their [material] interests as between themselves, and as against other men [and women] whose interests are different from (and usually opposed to) theirs" (Thompson, 1964: 9). This does not mean, of course, that this context unproblematically reflects the dominant,

Marxist paradigm of processes of class formation. There is no doubt, in fact, that Papua New Guinea was a place with some distinctively Melanesian ways.[14]

In effect, in Papua New Guinea the conjunction between class and experience (between an objectively defined set of economically derived positions and subjectively held identities – between class "of itself" and class "for itself"), though increasingly important, was only partial (see Joyce, 1995; Scott, 1995; Stedman Jones, 1995). This was so in part because a sharp polarization between owners and workers (a polarization that would contribute to the creation of materially based, oppositional interests) did not seem likely to exist in Papua New Guinea (but see Amarshi, Good and Mortimer, 1979; Thompson and MacWilliam, 1992). (To be sure, such a conjunction, as Lukács [1971] and others have noted, is far from inevitable, even with such a sharp polarization.)

Such a polarization did not exist for several reasons. The first was that, while there were the affluent and the poor, these were not owners and workers in the classic sense. As stated, in an economic circumstance of large-scale, foreign and governmentally owned projects of resource extraction, few Papua New Guineans (those readily defined as the upper class) actually controlled much of the means of production. Certainly in Wewak, the most affluent and influential either owned retail businesses (often small-to-medium in size) or worked as professionals for themselves or for the government. And, few Papua New Guineans actually had to sell their labor to survive. This was the case despite the fact that about 20 percent of Papua New Guineans lived in the towns[15] and unemployment was high. Since little land (only about 3 percent) had been alienated permanently, many town dwellers could (likely) still return home to a viable, subsistence economy (see O'Faircheallaigh, 1992; cf. Fitzpatrick, 1980).

The second reason for the absence of such a polarization, which might have furthered a consonance between class of itself and for itself, was that the elite (consisting, once again, largely of the middle class) and the grass roots, in fact, still shared significant overlapping interests. In a country where there were over 700 different linguistic groups, the distinctions between affluent and poor still were at least partially cross-cut by ethnic allegiances which continued to provide traditional sources of identities and interests (see Fitzpatrick, 1980; May, 1984; Turner, 1990).[16] Most Chambri, hence, whether the handful in the middle class or the majority in the grass roots, still identified themselves as importantly Chambri. (However, as we shall indicate, those of the middle class were increasingly transforming and attenuating their ties with coculturalists.)

Moreover, affluent and poor shared some commonalities, not only because identities and corresponding interests complexly mingled traditional and modernist elements, but because such modernist elements were themselves variable and various. Thus, some of the modernist ways in which many Papua New Guineans – whether affluent or poor – were defining their identities and interests were both shifting and multifaceted: virtually all were exploring and appropriating imported activities ranging in general accessibility from evangelical religions and bingo to golf and Rotary.

Finally, and significantly, to the extent that identities and interests were defined in terms of a modernist (capitalist) economy, they tended (as with bingo, golf and Rotary) to reflect the capacity to consume rather than the capacity to produce (see Philibert, 1989). Taken together, these particularities of Papua New Guinea suggest that the new inequalities should, to some extent, be understood in terms of a Weberian view of status, one focused on lifestyle (see, especially, Weber, 1968).[17]

Weber clearly differentiated class relations from status relations: "classes are stratified according to their relations to the production and acquisition of goods; whereas status groups are stratified according to the principles of their *consumption* of goods as represented by special styles of life" (1968: 937). Yet, despite this analytic differentiation, he well recognized that status disparities could be closely "knit" to a class situation. Indeed, in our view, such was very much the case in Papua New Guinea. There the elite had a socioeconomically based set of identities and interests focused on the capacity to consume and to display in a culturally salient manner. In other words, the elite were able to distinguish themselves from the grass roots primarily through their superior access to the money that in turn provided them with a restricted and sought-after lifestyle (see, especially, Parkin, 1979).[18] Hence, as central to understanding new processes of distinction, we examine members of the emerging and largely urban middle-class elite, with respect not only to their key economic positions, but also to their successful embodiment of a coveted lifestyle.[19]

This lifestyle had become coveted for various reasons. Perhaps the most important was that it had become synonymous with "development," and development had long been used by colonists and first-world others to distinguish themselves as superior and to justify their superiority, both on an individual and a collective level. Development, whether enabling individuals to enjoy particularly affluent and prestigious lifestyles or enabling whole collectivities to command high standards of living and deference, had been presented as deserved – as reflecting both personal industry and rational (modernist) institutional arrangements.

Such a perspective on the perquisites and conditions of development was promulgated, for example, during the late colonial period by the Reserve Bank of Australia, in association with Australian-owned banks then operating in Papua New Guinea. In a series of pamphlets designed "for use by [Papua New Guinean] secondary school children and others who want to learn something about money and saving" (*Your Money*, n.d.: i), the desire for wealth was presented as "natural because we all like to make progress and have a better standard of living" (*What is Wealth?*, n.d.: 8). These pamphlets also answered the question of why some individuals fulfilled this natural desire more completely than others by referring to hard and efficient work. In essence, those who had the wealth to sustain an affluent lifestyle deserved it:

> Some people do not understand how richer persons get good homes, motor cars, refrigerators, radios and furniture while other people who also work hard, still have to live in small huts.
>
> The people who own these things have got them ... by saving, by working and earning money, by growing crops for sale, by raising livestock, by trading or by obtaining them from relatives. Most of them have worked hard but also efficiently. People train as Teachers and Government officials. Others train as Doctors, Lawyers or Engineers, and so on. They earn more money in this way because of their training. Other people train as organisers of businesses and factories so that they can also earn more money.
>
> In every country of the world, there have always been some people who are more wealthy than other people. (*What is Wealth?*, n.d.: 9-10).

Moreover, in both implicit and explicit opposition to the European self-representations of their money-based economic system as rational, reasonable, fair, natural and leading to progress in the form of development, was the native system. Throughout the pamphlets, in fact, Papua New Guinea's indigenous systems were portrayed as curtailing progress – as fundamentally unproductive in a narrow materialist sense – because they channeled wealth into the ownership of pigs and the staging of feasts; conversely, the indigenous systems did not encourage appropriately focused savings or investment. Thus, of the nine "main ways of increasing wealth in the Territory [of Papua New Guinea]" with which *What is Wealth?* concluded, the first was: "Saving by people so that savings can be put to some purpose which is productive" (20).

Native economic systems were, as well, presented as cumbersome and inefficient in the modern world:

> Can you imagine the difficulty in exchanging, at a shop or a store, a pig for a radio set or a guitar? Even if you could bring the pig to the shop or store which had the radio set or guitar for sale, the shopkeeper might not want the pig. However, he would always accept money. Besides, the pig might not be worth the same as the radio set or guitar, so how would you settle the difference in value? (*Your Money*, n.d.: 2)

The colonial encounters that such development-oriented rhetoric encapsulated have had their lasting effects. This is well conveyed in Kulick's moving account of a Gapun villager's understanding of what was for him, and for most of the grass roots, Papua New Guinea's continuing, postcolonial collective backwardness:

> "[I]t's like we want to come up like all European countries. In the countries you've all changed ... In the countries everyone lives well ... And, too, you've got all kinds of factories to make all kinds of things: boats or ships or airplanes or cars or motors or money – whatever, all these factories are in the countries. There aren't any here among us in Papua New Guinea. We're the last country. And the way of life, too. In the countries it's good. There's no work. Like what we do here – carry heavy things around on our shoulders, walk around through the jungle like pigs. No. You all just sit, drive around in cars. It's the same with food. White people just eat tinned food, everything comes in a tin – tinned fish or tinned meat or tinned crab or tinned shrimp – whatever, it all comes in a tin. Houses. You all live in good houses. They have rooms in them, toilets. But us here, no. We haven't come up a little bit." (quoted in Kulick, 1992: 55).

Obviously, development has remained both highly desirable and, for most, painfully elusive. Comparatively few Papua New Guineans could drive around in cars and live in good houses. And with educational and employment opportunities ever more limited, there seemed slight chance for enlarging the middle class (AusAid, 1995).[20] Those already in the middle class, as teachers, bureaucrats and businesspeople, not only controlled access to educational and employment opportunities (Moore, 1990; Johnson, 1993; Romaine, 1995), they also had a pivotal role as the obvious and ostensibly emulatable embodiments of development (and, as such, the admired heirs of the colonists). Indeed – and importantly – the middle class had become the evident and envied exemplars[21] of the "material lifestyles and ideologies" (Hau'ofa, 1987: 11) conveyed in mass advertising as constitutive of a "normal" – developed – life (Errington and Gewertz, 1996; Foster, 1997). They, more than any others in Papua New Guinea, seemed able to fulfill a "natural" desire for affluence and – as we shall see throughout this book – to validate themselves as deserving of that affluence.

Thus, in Papua New Guinea, members of the middle class could accurately be regarded as a major factor in "energising and transforming civil society" (Hooper, n.d.: 22). They were a major factor in reclassifying identities and interests – in reclassifying who people were, what they were worth and what they sought to effect. Postcolonial Papua New Guinea was, in other words, hardly a place where, as Narakobi had hoped, an affluent person would not regard "[t]he person dressed in rags . . . as an inferior being" (1980: 31).

Because our principal concern is to utilize the anthropological knowledge acquired through long-term fieldwork to convey the significance of a major shift in the nature of relationships, many of the economic and geopolitical influences affecting the growth of the Papua New Guinean middle class remain peripheral to this study. Thus, we do not deal directly and systematically with a number of factors pertinent to class formation, including the detailed workings of the Papua New Guinea political economy: the country's strategies for tariffs and crop subsidies; its use of price-stabilization funds; its arrangements with international lending institutions; its formulation and enforcement of banking and tax policies; its utilization of investment incentives; its educational policies for the creation of an elite (but see Thompson and MacWilliam, 1992). Nor, finally, do we explore government and commerce at the highest levels, those at which national and international negotiations, deals and socialities were effected.

Instead, we primarily convey in fine-grained ethnographic detail how social and cultural forms of *enduring* inequality were experienced, justified, and propagated. We mean, in so doing, to compel recognition (and, once again, among readers who include Westerners accustomed to the naturalization of class differences) of the often

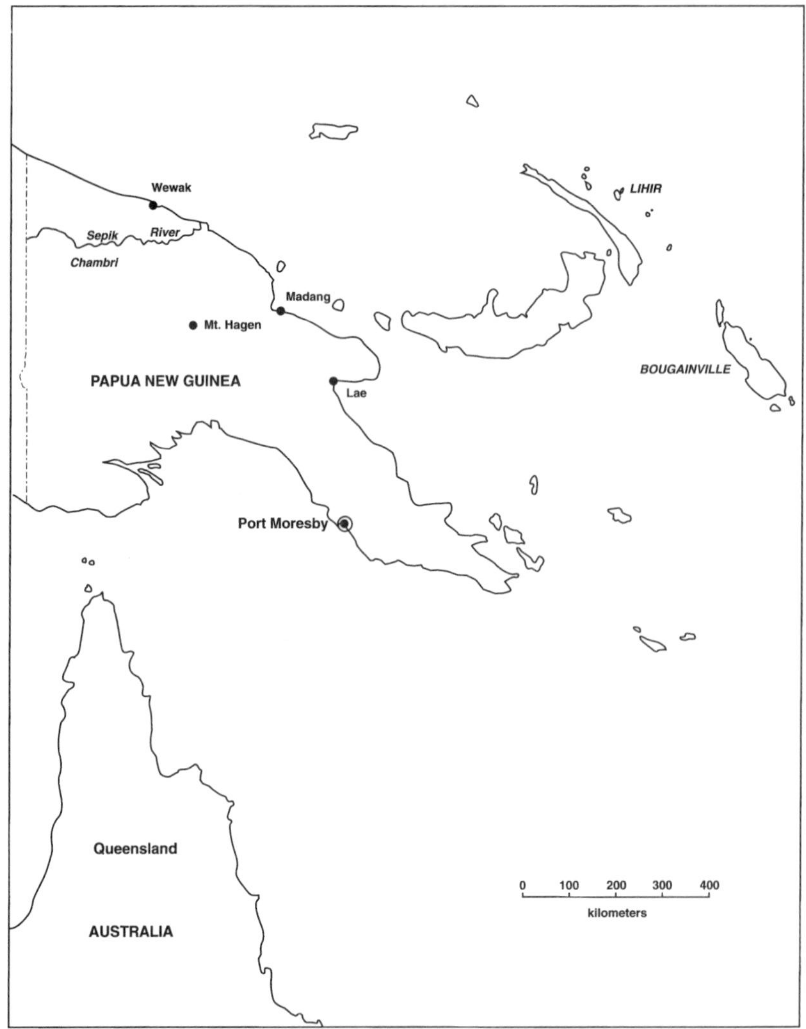

Map 1. The places mentioned in this book.

beguiling ways in which practices and policies of exclusion could be presented as thoroughly appropriate – presented not simply as the product of class interests, but as inevitable and fair. Our concern, in other words, is with the capitalist sleights of hand – albeit, and importantly, with distinctive cultural twists – by which the slights inherent in such statements of relative worth have been conveyed with significant effect in Papua New Guinea and, perhaps, elsewhere.

1. Wewak was a town of some 50,000 inhabitants. These were mostly nationals – both squatters with uncertain incomes and those with more secure residence and regular jobs.

Our work

Our information about class distinctions in Papua New Guinea has come largely, but not exclusively, from our research in Wewak. While our research was not designed to generate an ethnography of Wewak (but see Gewertz and Errington, 1991a: 101–125), the ethnographic knowledge we had gained about the town from our several studies of Chambri living, visiting and coping there certainly proved useful – and in several senses. It convinced us that Wewak would be an appropriate site for our study of class formation insofar as it was reasonably typical of medium-sized Papua New Guinea commercial centers. (On Papua New Guinean cities, see Connell and Lea, 1993; see, as well, Strathern, 1975; Levine and Levine, 1979; Battaglia, 1995.)

It was a town of, by some estimates, 50,000 inhabitants. Most were nationals (both squatters with uncertain incomes[22] and those with more secure residences and regular jobs) drawn from all over Papua New Guinea, although most heavily from the surrounding province. As well, there were perhaps 350 "expats": largely Chinese,

2. We were able to arrange in advance for accommodation in a neighborhood of affluent Papua New Guineans.

Australian, Filipino, and European entrepreneurs, missionaries, and technical advisors. Wewak did, to be sure, have less evident extremes of wealth and a smaller industrial base than, for example, Port Moresby and Lae (the country's two largest cities, where those few Papua New Guineans possessing real capital were likely to live and work). Nor, like Mount Hagen, was it the center of a flourishing cash-cropping region. But, it did have an active port (filled with foreign-owned fishing boats), an international airport (with flights throughout the country and to Indonesia), warehouses for the processing and purveying of coffee and cacao, and depots for oil and gas. In addition, like most Papua New Guinea provincial towns, it had some tourist-related service industries, many wholesale and retail operations and an extensive civil service.

Moreover, our prior knowledge of, and connections to, Wewak did help us establish ourselves there among the middle class. We were, thus, able to arrange in advance for accommodation in a neighborhood of affluent Papua New Guineans: next to our house (owned by a Chinese entrepreneur), for instance, was one owned by Westpac Bank as a residence for its local bank manager (a national). Finally, living in Wewak enabled us to continue focused work with the

3. Our interviews were often conducted at our house, at our informant's workplace, or at a restaurant.

Chambri, especially concerning how the happenings of class were – for the most part, adversely – affecting them.

In order to understand how members of the middle class positioned themselves in relationship to others in contemporary Papua New Guinea, we formally interviewed eighty-eight of the more affluent of Wewak's middle-class nationals: 56 men and 32 women (including 8 Chambri men and 1 Chambri woman). They were lawyers, doctors, nurses, bankers, clergy, teachers, managers, entrepreneurs, shopkeepers, army personnel, civil servants. Each interview, usually conducted at our home, at our informant's workplace, or at a restaurant, lasted between one and three hours. We asked a relatively consistent set of questions, designed to reveal how these members of the middle class defined themselves, both through their social connections and through their social disconnections. Thus, first we explored aspects of life histories to learn where they and their parents had been born, raised and educated (as, for instance, in villages or in towns). Then we probed the extent to which they defined themselves in relationship to kin, coworkers and the members of churches and clubs to which they belonged. We would ask, for example, where, how, and with whom they had spent the last few weekends. Conversely, we would ask about likely areas where their obligations had shifted or become attenuated: when had they last visited their home villages; when, if at all, had they contributed to such traditional responsibilities as death ceremonies; if they could speak an indigenous language and, if so, were they teaching that language to their children; and how had they dealt with the inevitable and potentially ruinous demands of less affluent kin.

In addition to conducting these interviews, we plunged into Papua New Guinean middle-class life in a variety of contexts, including the Rotary, golf and yacht clubs. There (and elsewhere) we socialized frequently, significantly thickening our knowledge of middle-class life. We participated in special club-centered functions (such as annual fundraisers, which often included betting events as on the Melbourne Cup, and semiformal dinner dances); we went regularly to Catholic and Assembly of God church services and church-focused gatherings (such as those of Catholic neighborhood organizations known as "Little Christian Communities"); we engaged in political rallies concerning law-and-order issues (during one, our house was robbed, which, in turn, involved us with middle-class insurance agents); we lectured at the local teacher's college (and were kindly given a set of essays that students – many of them, middle-class aspirants, if not descendants – had written about their own cultural groups); we participated in an organization to promote Sepik women in trade; and we attended Chamber of Commerce meetings (one was convened for a visit of the Parliamentary Minister of Commerce and Industry). Moreover, we volunteered once a week as English-language reading tutors at Wewak's (private) International School, where we met with many of the children of our middle-class friends and where the Papua New Guinean headmaster allowed us to survey parents concerning the educational and professional aspirations they had for their children.[23] In short, our chapters convey what we learned in a range of contexts about emerging class distinctions in contemporary Papua New Guinea life.

While many analysts of class formation have described the effects of socioeconomic transformations on social relations and the development of new kinds of identities and interests, these are generally historical reconstructions (see, especially, Thompson, 1964).[24] What we show is how these new inequalities, the distinctions of incommensurability, were becoming lived – and in a place, as we have said, generally characterized by a strenuously egalitarian ethos. Each of our chapters, in fact, has been designed to portray aspects of the sometimes wrenching process whereby some were able to redefine the ontological worth of themselves and others.

Although the distinctions of incommensurability we document have been relatively novel in Papua New Guinea, they have been conveyed in part through social forms having long and still viable histories elsewhere. We strive, therefore, throughout the book to remain mindful that currents of global capitalism have affected Papua New Guinea. Indeed, as will be apparent, many of the forms and currents that have been reshaping Papua New Guinean lives have also figured importantly – if, given the passage of time, less conspicuously – in our own. For example, the Rotary Club's pioneering work of class formation in Papua New Guinea should be connected (both for self- and global understanding) to the solid, reliable, and familiar work it has long been doing in the United States (and elsewhere).

Since our primary ethnographic goal is to relate how certain discriminations have been actually employed to alter Papua New Guinean lives – their identities, interests and worths – we have written a compositely, rather than linearly, cumulative book. Through thick description of a range of encounters between those differentially positioned in the relationships of class, we seek to delineate crucial aspects of the way that class differences have been learned and experienced. We seek, in other words, to capture class as "a fluency which evades analysis if we attempt to stop it dead at any given moment and anatomize its structure ... [as a] relationship [which] must always be embodied in real people and in a real context" (Thompson, 1964: 9). Each of our chapters, therefore, focuses on particular sets of contexts and engagements through which the inclusions and exclusions – the connections and disconnections with past and present and with other Papua New Guineans – get told with telling effects.

In our first chapter, we introduce a template of sociality embraced by Wewak's affluent as they engaged with each other in such (largely) imported contexts as Rotary International. This template defined society as voluntarily constituted by like-minded and like-positioned individuals for their mutual benefit. In so doing, it correspondingly justified the attenuation of obligations between the affluent and their kin and coculturalists: it was an attenuation necessary for the achievement of middle-class interests and identities – for a lifestyle of affluence.

We show in our second chapter how key premises of middle-class sociality contributed to the promulgation of a particular understanding of the poor. In discussing a voluntary organization of middle-class women, created to assist impoverished women in marketing their handicrafts, we demonstrate how the poor became defined as constituting a distinct category – as "other" – and as responsible for their own poverty. In so defining the poor, the affluent could, with clear – indeed, Christian – conscience blame (while ostensibly helping) the victim.

Those so defined as "other" did not necessarily recognize the extent of the class barriers they confronted. In our third chapter, we describe the persistent efforts made by Godfried Kolly, a grass-roots Chambri friend, to achieve middle-class acceptance. Godfried strongly wanted his largely middle-class, fellow soccer referees to desire him and the imported soccer whistles he controlled. His oscillation between elation, bafflement, despair, resentment and hope over their responses to him is the story of his encounter with the increasingly categorical exclusions of class.

Michael Kamban, another grass-roots Chambri friend, was more clearly angry (and clearer about his anger) over class exclusion, and it is his story we tell in our fourth chapter. Here we provide the sharpest contrast – the sharpest clash – between the ways in which those of the grass roots and the middle class sought to constitute the social world. Our focus is on Wewak's Resort and Country Club, where Papua New Guinean golfers would, for example, have been more comfortable entertaining the multicultural (and American Express emissary) Tiger Woods than they would have been entertaining our angry friend.

In our fifth chapter, we examine the threat to social order that members of the middle class thought was emanating from the hostility of those of the grass roots. We describe a rally held to protest about the deterioration of law and order in Wewak and to enlist broad-based support for an end to violence and crime. While the opinions expressed were supposedly drawn from all sectors of a democratically constituted society, they actually sustained the middle-class perception that the ultimate cause of crime was the faulty socialization and unreasonable expectations of grass-roots youth.

In our final ethnographic chapter, we consider the widely publicized case of a young woman who had ostensibly been denied her civil rights when her kinsmen "sold" her as part of a traditional compensation. Here we show how middle-class perspectives, including those expressed in the law and order rally, have become institutionalized in Papua New Guinea's legal system. Not only have members of the middle class become the arbiters of reasonability, they have also made the lives of the grass roots, including their traditions, subject to judicial review.

In our conclusion, after speculating about the future of the middle class in Papua New Guinea, we present a brief cautionary tale concerning the twists and turns of difference likely to affect our own lives.

I

The middle class – the (new) Melanesian way

The Wewak Rotary Club

We begin our talk about the emerging nature of class distinction in contemporary Papua New Guinea life with discussion of a particularly salient set of contexts and engagements for forging the redefinitions central to the happenings of class: for creating new inclusions and exclusions through which the connections and disconnections with past and present and with other Papua New Guineans were reformulated. Our focus is Wewak's Rotary Club. A thoroughly middle-class, capitalist-based organization both in its American inception and its Papua New Guinean manifestation, Rotary facilitated efforts by members of Wewak's middle class to create and consolidate their new identities and interests. To understand this context of redefinition – of class happenings – we will explore what Rotary International, both as organizational form and ideology, brought with it to Papua New Guinea, what it has encountered there, and what it has produced.

The inception of Rotary as a middle-class institution

Rotary's worldwide career began in the United States in the early twentieth century. Its founder, Paul Harris, had come as a young lawyer to a Chicago characterized by daunting social anonymity and economic competition – features only exacerbated by the cut-throat impersonality of an increasingly powerful corporate capitalism.[1] Harris, realizing that others, too, lacked both friends and business contacts, undertook in 1905 to create a fellowship of those pledged to aid each other in business.[2] Believing that only noncompetitors (and one might add, class equals) could be friends, and sensing the advantage in having diverse business allies in what he hoped would be an economically fruitful network, he recruited for his club a single member (if possible, the most distinguished) from each of a range of occupations. Initially, in order to display their professional services, members hosted meetings in rotation (hence "Rotary") at their various business establishments.

In the ensuing several decades, Rotary expanded exponentially in the United States, with clubs in every major city by 1915. At the same time it spawned two direct competitors, Kiwanis and Lions, in 1915 and 1917. Clearly Harris' effort to deal with the isolation of atomized individuals in highly competitive entrepreneurial capitalism was appealing, particularly to middle-class, small-scale businessmen and professionals. Providing an essentially conservative way of working within the existing system – of prospering within rather than opposing or significantly transforming the system – the Harris model of sociality might be viewed as Durkheimian rather than Marxist.

Indeed, given its continuing insistence on its "classification system" – there being *one* representative from each occupation – Rotary remained fundamentally premised on an organic solidarity. This solidarity took full cognizance of an advanced division of labor and the existence of occupational enclaves. At the same time, it sought to avoid the potential anomie deriving from the insularism of occupational enclaves. Yet because Rotary also sought the *best* representative from each occupation, it relied on the continuing activities of these occupational enclaves in fostering professional excellence. Thus, eschewing any Marxist idea of an explosively riven society, Rotary – in its middle-class, and perhaps Panglossian, aspirations – hoped that its, in effect, Durkheimian minisociety was also a Weberian (medium-high) status group.

Its members were prosperous, influential and respectable, yet rarely truly elite. The center of gravity in the Rotarian microcosm consequently remained in the middle or upper middle class – with managers of small-scale businesses and with professionals. As such, and perhaps as a continuation of its Midwestern cultural roots, its ambiance also remained friendly and informal – neighborly.[3] However, for reasons additional to the fact that the social extremes were either not recruited or did not join, Rotary never fulfilled its organizational premise of becoming an organic whole. Members early on concluded they were restricting themselves to a less than viable sphere, especially since they were obligated to give each other favorable terms. In short, they needed outside business. Therefore, Rotary had to look outwards to cultivate economic relationships with non-Rotarians.

Members were also sensitive to charges of social isolation. Clearly influenced by the ideals of the Progressive Era, Rotarians began to concern themselves with issues of social welfare, such as the need of underprivileged children for recreational facilities. Reflecting this social concern, they coined the motto which persists today: "Service above self." Yet, perhaps a more accurate motto might have been, "Service *and* self."

Rotary as a "service organization" could be regarded as a strategic expansion of its founder's vision of a community in which sociability and profit were equally legitimate and necessary. Thus, another Rotary slogan, first uttered in a keynote address delivered at the national convention in 1911, became, "He profits most who serves best." In this view, it was good business to do a good job, as by serving customers well, and it was good business to do good more generally, as by contributing time and money to community projects. In other words, businessmen could expect to flourish from the patronage of their satisfied and prosperous neighbors. Furthermore, this slogan reflected a view in which public good was synonymous with good capitalism, a capitalism that was small-scale and personal, middle-class and noncorporate. And, of course, in such a community context, fellow Rotarians would remain important social and business contacts.

Rotary soon became international. Expanding first to Canada and then to the British Isles (where by 1912 there were ten clubs), its global expansion (initially, though not exclusively, throughout the English-speaking world) accelerated greatly after World War One. Rotary arrived in Wewak, a long way from the first Chicago club, in 1965. At the time of our research in 1996, the Wewak club was one of ten in Papua New Guinea, all clubs belonging to District 9600. (District 9600 included seventy clubs: those in Papua New Guinea, the Solomon Islands and also in part of Queensland, including Brisbane.)

In understanding the Wewak Rotary Club, the problem we faced was not so much to explain why Rotary had flourished among white (mostly Australian) expatriates during the 1960s. After all, there were more similarities between the heartland of early twentieth-century America and the periphery of the Antipodes a half-century later than might at first be expected. The American citizens who, for instance, thronged to world's fairs celebrating the global triumph of material progress and control were not that different in their middle-class expectations and aspirations[4] from those Australians who sought a convivial and affluent life in business or government during the economic prosperity of Papua New Guinea's post World War Two colonial period. Both these Americans and Australians felt justified in, and validated by, the extension of their particular way of life to the rest of the world. In a world laid open for business, it seemed that prosperity *appropriately* went to those who also served – those who provided "uplift," whether through building playgrounds or shouldering the "white man's burden."

Rather, our analytic problem became how to explain Rotary's persistence in Wewak – and by extension, Papua New Guinea – in a postcolonial time marked by economic decline and a widespread shift of important jobs from noncitizens to citizens. What was Rotary's consonance with Wewak's middle class – both emerging and remnant? How, for instance, did the concept of service-above-self manifest itself there? And what were the broader socioeconomic implications of Rotary's existence in a rapidly transforming Papua New Guinea?

On Wewak's middle class and its Rotarian "chiefs"

Wewak's Rotary Club was one of Papua New Guinea's smaller ones, with twelve members during 1996. Six were Papua New Guinean nationals and six, expats: one Chinese and five Europeans (including the two of us).[5] In fact, according to membership figures in the *Governor's Newsletter*, published by District 9600, there were at this time only about 250 active Rotarians in the whole of Papua New Guinea. However, because members conspicuously worked for the public good and represented widely held middle-class values and aspirations, Rotary's significance, both in Papua New Guinea generally and in Wewak in particular, was greater than these numbers might suggest.

Certainly Rotary was well known for its commitment to service. For example, when the Port Moresby club on 22 May 1996 flew Papua New Guinean Siamese twins (with their parents) from Papua New Guinea to Melbourne for surgical separation, Rotary was lauded throughout Papua New Guinea and Australia. And, in Wewak alone, Rotary reached thousands through its service activities. Also, as we shall see, the Wewak Rotary Club successfully persuaded many of the town's several hundred middle-class nationals and expats to participate in its fund-raising efforts.

There could be no doubt that the restricted membership and affluent sociability of Rotary – as well as that of the larger, purely recreational golf and yacht clubs, with paid-up memberships of 60 and 85 respectively – provided a desired exclusiveness for some members of the middle class. Though Rotary was smaller than either the golf or yacht clubs, many of Wewak's middle class found its combination of exclusive fellowship and commitment to service especially appealing. Indeed, attendance at the twice-monthly Rotary meetings was often substantially augmented by guests, some of whom were prospective members. Yet membership was very expensive – sometimes too much so – in both money and time.

In fact, we met both nationals and expats who told us that they had appreciated Rotary, but, after a few meetings, had found participation difficult to afford. It was not just the yearly dues of K90.00 (one kina was equivalent to US$.80) that discouraged them from joining or continuing their membership. Monthly dinners cost K15.00 and fines for minor infractions of Rotary rules – such as coming late to a meeting (although minimal in comparison to fines in Rotary Clubs elsewhere) – mounted up. Most financially draining, and key to fulfilling the standards of the affluent sociability that constituted Rotary's fellowship, were standing rounds of drinks. We, for instance, would return home from a dinner meeting full of fellowship but depleted of funds, having spent K60–80.00. Even an ordinary business meeting typically cost us K25–30.00. Early on, when we semijokingly mentioned to the club's president, an affluent national physician, that we had to visit the bank prior to Rotary meetings, he jovially remarked that a Rotarian should not complain about the cost of anything, especially not of Rotary: he should enjoy his job, and enjoy earning and spending money on fellowship and on service.

Though Wewak's Rotarians sometimes complained that service was not a value easily adopted by all nationals (or, for that matter, all expats – whether, for instance, Chinese or European), we found that service was, at least rhetorically, valued by a significant number of Wewak's middle-class nationals. Even some of the same persons criticized by Rotarians as unduly self-focused would offer examples of community service. One national woman, for example, explained her own intense preoccupation with her multifaceted business by mentioning with pride her father's signal contribution to the economic and social development of Wewak and Papua New Guinea more generally. (We will meet her again as our golf partner in chapter 3.) Another national, a businessman, justifying his preoccupation with his own affairs, stressed the generous financial assistance he regularly gave to local fund-raising activities, including those of Rotary. (More will be said about these activities later.)

Indeed, we were struck by how similar the six nationals active in Rotary – five men and one woman – were to the dozens of other members of Wewak's middle class with whom we spoke at length. One was a physician in private practice; one, a bank manager; one, a high school headmaster; one, the International School's headmaster; one, a trade store owner; one – the only national woman – an administrator of the province's "youth" office. They came from various provinces and ethnic groups in Papua New Guinea. Four married outside of their cultural groups. Only three spoke their native languages well and not one regularly spoke a native language in his/her home (even in the two cases in which both spouses spoke the same native language). All were fluent in English and had completed tertiary education. Many sent, or intended to send, their children to the International School so that they might learn, as one Rotarian put it, the "non-Melanesian inflected English which would allow them to become competitive in a world market." As the children of fathers who themselves worked for the government or for missions, none had been brought up in villages.

Significantly, and again, in a manner completely typical of the many national middle-class business and professional people to whom we spoke, all nationals in Rotary stressed the complexity of their relationships with grass-roots relatives who, as less affluent and educated, were different in a variety of ways. All recognized that kin demands for economic assistance, such as to pay school fees, or engage in ritual activities, or just to hang-out in town, could mean financial ruin unless properly controlled.[6] Most had established stringent rules to regulate these demands, lest they be "pulled down" to the grass-roots level. They explained to their kin that they could only occasionally help with more than a few kina and, then, primarily for some worthy purpose such as school or hospital fees. Many stressed that they sought to educate their kin to "respect" the demands and complexities of their middle-class lifestyles – to recognize and accept that they had to meet their own considerable expenses, which ranged from restocking their stores to buying toilet paper for their families.

In fact, though, they often did finance ceremonies in their home villages, particularly death rituals for senior kinsmen. Yet, they regarded this less as a commitment to tradition than as an investment. Knowing little of ritual specifics or attendant cosmology, they participated financially largely to strengthen their future claims on ancestral land – land they explicitly referred to as an "asset." At the same time, they resented being asked by villagers to contribute to ceremonial work. They thought the villagers were making an extractive business out of such rituals and so "draining resources" better used in other ways.

One Rotary member, for example, who still resided on ancestral land only a few miles from Wewak, had for years accepted his mother's advice as to which of his ritual obligations were mandatory. Nevertheless, despite the thousands of kina he expended – money he wanted to invest in the expansion of his in-town office complex – he still bitterly quarreled with his kinsmen. Most recently, he and his siblings had sought without success to convince their cousins to grant them full ownership of their share of ancestral land so that they might develop it without further consultation or claims. So strained were relations that he was reluctant to drive at night: he was afraid his cousins, resentful of his success and wishing to maintain their collective power over him and his family, might throw rocks at his van or, more likely, hire someone to attack him or his vehicle.

Yet, even as interactions with grass-roots kin became increasingly instrumental and as customary practices – generally concerning life-cycle rituals and land tenure – became redefined in a pervasively cash economy, few of the middle class wished to give up entirely their cultural identity. They still (at least when asked) defined themselves as members of a particular ethnic group, although, significantly, they might joke, disparagingly, that they were not one of those "bushy Boiken." Certainly, at the very least, they defined themselves as, for instance, "Sepiks." Most held a genuine interest in their traditions, although this interest had become limited and ambivalent.

Thus, one Rotary member with political aspirations (whose activities we discuss again in chapter 5), an Arapesh by birth, asked us to send her the three-volume set of Margaret Mead's *The Mountain Arapesh* (1970). She, like many members of the middle class with whom we spoke, had grown up away from her cultural group and hence was largely ignorant of her traditions. Prompted both by a diffuse personal curiosity about her "roots" and by a more pressing political need to convince village people that she was still located in her culture, she wished to acquire distinctive cultural authority. Indeed, she sought a kind of cultural connection which would, in effect, elevate her over others in her cultural group. Hence, if elected as representative of her constituency, she would have both connection and separation.

Importantly, the particular articulation of connection and separation provided a frequent justification for developing class distinctions, a justification with a neocolonial, Melanesian twist. All of Wewak's Papua New Guinean Rotarians – and most others in Wewak's emergent middle class – often spoke about themselves in ways that strongly implied an inevitable superiority because of ancestral precedent. Even those from among Papua New Guinea's most competitively egalitarian groups would describe their fathers not as "big men" but as "chiefs," that is, as hereditary leaders. To be sure, their fathers may well have been prominent, possessing more of what others had: pigs, pearl shells, ritual knowledge, wives, and land. After all, the practices of colonial administration, such as installing local leaders as headmen, may have dampened fluctuating inequalities to the extent that the momentarily influential could ensure educational and other forms of "advancement" for themselves and their children.[7] Yet, perhaps not surprisingly, our middle-class informants saw their distinction more as the product of ontology than of historical caprice or process. They were separated as permanently privileged because they were of a "chiefly" line.[8]

This modern-day rhetoric of "chiefs" was, in fact, proving increasingly useful to politicians in particular and to members of the middle class in general, to justify growing class differences (see, for comparison, Feinberg, 1978; Besnier, 1996; Howard, 1996; Lutkehaus, 1996; White and Lindstrom, 1998). It summarized and made more palatable the shifts in life's opportunities that everyone knew were taking place. It presented a transformed present in terms of a reinvented, stable past which defined distinction not in terms of continuity but of difference. It also implied that difference still carried certain, though distinctly limited, obligations. Thus, unlike big men (again, who were like everyone else but more so), contemporary "chiefs" were clearly different, at least partially – though not completely – dissociated. This, we think, both signaled and facilitated a shift in political process in the direction of increasing stratification. The big man's compulsory egalitarian and leveling redistribution to his allies was becoming transformed: it was changing into the politician's discretionary handouts to his electorate (such handouts, drawn mostly at election time from large slush funds, were perhaps a form of stratified redistribution) as well as into the middle-class Rotarian's voluntary service – diffuse *noblesse oblige* – to the generalized less fortunate.[9]

Kinsmen and constituents did not, of course, overlook this attenuation of the ties between themselves and their leaders: kinsmen complained that their middle-class relatives had "turned their backs" on them; constituents complained that they never saw their politicians except before an election (as we shall see in chapter 3). From the perspective of the Rotarian, and other middle-class "chiefs," however, this attenuation freed resources which could not only be invested in business and family but in relations with one another as useful class equals. Harris and his subsequent Rotarians combined sociality with business; so also did Wewak's Rotary Club members. They bought each other drinks, dined together, and gave each other business assistance and advice, including somewhat privileged information. True, Rotarians (as did others in the middle class) cultivated their own networks. They kept up, for instance, with university classmates and with colleagues met elsewhere, including those met during training abroad. Nonetheless, Rotary was particularly important to them. Members talked about how useful Rotary was, how well-placed Rotarians were both locally and more generally. Indeed, one Rotarian jokingly described Rotary International as an "extremely effective Mafia."

Part of the importance to these middle-class nationals of their Rotary networks, we came to understand, stemmed from the fact that Rotary was not only inherited from expats, but still included them. Furthermore, these middle-class nationals cherished the fact that the Wewak club remained part of the worldwide organization of clubs constituting Rotary International.[10]

Wewak Rotary in – and as – a world system

Simply put, in postcolonial Wewak, the expat members of Rotary remained important arbiters of the degree to which national members were not just economically and socially advantaged relative to other Papua New Guineans but were superior, having not just cash but cultivation. At the time of our research, these expat members were: the male, Australian owner of a company selling portable sawmills and exporting tropical hardwoods; the male,

French manager of the Catholic Mission's large wholesale and retail business; the female, Chinese–Australian manager of her family's wholesale and retail business; the female, British head of a program to educate teachers of the disabled; and two American anthropologists (having only their labor to sell!) – who, shortly before their departure, were replaced by two, married Canadian volunteers. (These volunteers had recently been assigned to Wewak to aid a women's organization in accounting and in marketing.) All (even in their way, the anthropologists) saw themselves as generally low-key, supportive mentors of the national Rotarians.

Often through example or discussion of established Rotary Club procedure and etiquette, subtleties of middle-class European lifestyles and standards were conveyed (see Bourdieu, 1977).[11] Thus, the expat Rotarians would clarify how to engage in nonpartisan good works (as with an even-handed distribution of the children's books received from an Australian Rotary Club); how to approach a fellow businessperson with a civic appeal (as in eliciting a contribution to the annual fund-raiser); how to entertain at home (as with providing drinks and hors-d'œuvre during the occasional unofficial meeting, always held in expat homes); how to maintain accounts and fiscal reputation (as with paying Rotary bills promptly); how to exhibit gracious manners (as in writing thank-you notes to other clubs which had offered toasts to one's own). The "instruction" was apparently accepted without resentment and, in fact, meetings seemed warm and fellowship, generous. This sociability assumed that the ontological difference between these "chiefs" and the grass roots was such that Wewak's Papua New Guinean Rotarians could, with a modicum of polishing, meet international standards. Indeed, the sociability indicated to them that membership in Rotary itself was both the means to, and the measure of, such acceptability.

In their turn, the national members of Wewak's Rotary Club helped the expat members deal with some of the generic difficulties foreigners were likely to encounter. Virtually everyone – expat and national alike – who engaged in business in Papua New Guinea met with difficulties. But the expats, in particular, found what they considered to be the poor roads, unreliable labor, inefficient and corrupt bureaucracy, and ever-present problems of protecting person and property from attack especially frustrating. Many expats to whom we talked wondered openly whether they had remained in the country too long and, in outstaying the late colonial prosperity, had fallen behind those who had remained at home. Rotary did in a very real way provide its expat members with useful connections which could help them do business with nationals in what was for them a trying context.

Rotary helped expats in another crucial regard. It helped them improve their public image. The expats not only considered themselves to be struggling against adverse circumstances but, as noncitizens engaged in business, to be vulnerable to accusations of exploitation, accusations which some feared could lead to deportation. Thought to have made large profits and to have invested them abroad, they were widely regarded as having no real connection with or commitment to the country or its people. Rotary counteracted this problem. It enabled its expat members to demonstrate to each other and to the public that expats and nationals could work productively together and socialize comfortably with each other. Moreover, it demonstrated to all that they could work not just for the benefit of themselves or other Rotarians, but for the betterment of the country.

The idea that Wewak's Rotary Club was part of Rotary International, a worldwide organization, was appealing to both its national and expat members. This was so in part because they all recognized that Papua New Guinea was peripheral as a third world nation. Certainly Wewak's Rotarians stressed that they were part of a community composed of millions of Rotarians: wherever they might find themselves, they were ensured of a welcome, of fellowship and assistance, from other Rotarians. Attesting to this fact and following standard Rotary practice, the Wewak Rotarians displayed at their meetings club banners from Australia, Japan, France, and the United States, as well as elsewhere in Papua New Guinea. These had been obtained by (mostly expat) members during visits to those clubs in exchange for Wewak Club banners. Comparably, and following standard Rotary protocol, Wewak Rotarians often proposed and reciprocated toasts linking them with other clubs.

In addition, many of Wewak's Rotarians would eagerly peruse and respond to the *District 9600 Newsletter* and the *Rotary Down Under* magazine, as distributed by the club's secretary. Once, for instance, an article describing the annual International Convention to be held in Calgary was discussed, with both national and expat members expressing a desire to attend. On another occasion, a national hoped that after the forthcoming fund-raiser, the Wewak club could make a generous contribution to the district's (Australian) governor for one of his special projects described in the newsletter. Similarly, an expat suggested sending a letter of support and condolence, as suggested in the newsletter, to the Hobart Rotary Club in Tasmania, reeling from the massacre at nearby Port Arthur.[12] As one final example: an expat described to other interested members his pleasure at the warm response he had received from the Rotary Club in his Australian home town. In fact, through his efforts, the Nedlands Club, made up largely of wealthy professionals, was sending the Wewak Rotarians many medical supplies for distribution to the less fortunate of the province.

Thus, as an international organization, Rotary provided assurance to the nationals that they had come up to the international standard;[13] it provided assurance to the expats that they had not fallen below that standard.[14] For them both, Rotary furnished the international connections as well as the context for service which ensured that all could unite as exemplars within a contemporary Papua New Guinea.

It was at their annual dinner-auction that these Rotarians most directly engaged comparable others in their vision of a desirable and achievable sociality. (This was a sociality achieved, as well, at golf functions, as we shall see in chapter 3.) This event brought together those of similar identities and interests so as to evoke a community of the middle-class residents of Papua New Guinea committed to a lifestyle in which good fellowship, good business and good works were seamlessly and without contradiction combined. The Wewak Rotarians, through their initiative and example, were thus emulating Paul Harris. They were crystallizing from the ambience of a world-capitalist culture both consciousness and substantiation of what it took for the middle class to thrive: a convincingly universalized, seemingly practical, pleasing vision, as well as enactment, of the right and proper. Of doing well by doing good.

Exemplary exchange: the annual Rotary dinner-auction

On the evening of 22 June 1996 selected members of the public began arriving for one of the Wewak Rotary Club's dinner meetings. As usual, it was held in the dining room of the New Wewak Hotel, on this occasion festooned with balloons. This dinner meeting was, however, to engage in some unusual, if annual business, as the decorations suggested. It was held to raise the money needed for the next year's service activities through the auction of donated goods and services. These goods and services had been solicited by

Rotarians, sometimes persistently, over a two-month period from commercial establishments in Wewak and beyond.

Eighty-one people spent 20K each to attend. By place of origin they were: 29 Papua New Guineans, 16 Chinese and Filipinos, and 35 Europeans. Although it was assumed that many of Wewak's expats would come as a matter of course, nationals were to be recruited, provided members could vouch for them. Central to the concerns of both nationals and expat Rotarians was that the national guests should not be rowdy and that they should have enough disposable income to bid generously. To this latter end, the auction was scheduled for a payday weekend, so that the nationals in particular would still have some of their fortnightly earnings to spend.

Guests arrived at the hotel's dining room in what the printed invitation had specified as "tropical formal dress": usually a white shirt and dark trousers for men, and a somewhat fancy frock for women. After milling about, chatting, buying drinks from the cash bar in a convivial, cocktail party manner, they examined the goods which Rotarians had earlier arranged into auction lots and placed in an impressive display at the front of the dining room. Then, the guests were seated for dinner and asked to check underneath their chairs in search of the two sticky labels indicating who had won free dinners at local eating establishments.

Guests were welcomed by the President of the Wewak Rotary Club, who was a national. In his address, he touched on the history of Rotary International and then on the founding of Wewak's club: it was begun in 1965 and, though still small, it was now healthy with twelve members. These members had, in accord with Rotary's motto of "Service above self," done much good work over the past few years. They had, for instance, renovated the building housing a literacy center for women, paid the correspondence course fees for worthy students from remote villages in the Province, provided an X-ray machine to a mission clinic and given books to local schools.

Then, as at all club meetings, the president proposed a toast to Queen Elizabeth II and to Papua New Guinea. Again in accord with club protocol, the International secretary proposed another toast to the Rotary Club of Amherst, Massachusetts as thanks for its contribution of $250 to the Wewak club's malaria control project. (This contribution, requested by the anthropologists, purchased inexpensive mosquito nets.) Next came the induction by the president and president-elect (the Papua New Guinean owner of a trade store) of two new members, the Canadian volunteers. Finally, the club's usual sort of formal business concluded, the dinner and conviviality began. This was the portion of Rotary gatherings given over to the explicit value of fellowship. The food was ample and conversation was animated.

Then came the main event: the auction. Following the club policy of "black/white" rotation, this year's auctioneer was the European manager of Boral Gas. (The other usual auctioneer, considered as good, was the Papua New Guinean head of security for a large Chinese-owned conglomerate.) Throughout, the auctioneer presented jokes evoking in-group knowledge. Beginning with reference to Rotary as a service organization, he announced a series of forthcoming public service lectures to be sponsored by the club and given by well-known local persons, whom he named. His announcements were greeted with howls of laughter. One lecture, entitled "Do It My Way," was to be given by a notoriously irascible European male golfer on golf etiquette; "Bali, Island of Love," was to be given by a European woman who had recently vacationed in Bali without her husband; and "Alcoholics Anonymous and How It Has Helped Me," was the title of lecture to be given by an absent and frequently deprecated Papua New Guinean politician.

This kind of dangerous humor was expected, and the auctioneer continued it throughout the evening. Once, for example, he alluded to a long-standing and fierce business competition between the two major Chinese wholesale operations in Wewak. This competition had, according to popular understanding, recently intensified with one firm reclaiming only with difficulty a shipping container of canned mackerel, worth about K45,000, which had ended up in the other's warehouse. Summoning the aggrieved owner of one firm and the representative of the other to the front of the room, the auctioneer presented an award for the best purveyor of gourmet food to the aggrieved owner. Looping a necklace of completely ordinary sausage links over his head and on to his immaculate white shirt, the auctioneer proclaimed the superiority of his firm's famous product. The auctioneer then handed the rival firm's representative a can of corned beef to present to the other in acknowledgment of the other's superior meats. As this spoof unfolded, the auctioneer pointedly stressed that it was meat and not fish being presented – thus invoking, through this humorously positive transaction in meat, the bitterly negative transaction in fish.

In addition, the auctioneer laced his bidding patter with ambiguously – sometimes dangerously – humorous jibes and other personal references. His evident strategy was to engage members of the audience by keeping them both amused and a bit off balance. Indeed, early on he announced that he would try to generate higher bids by creating contention rather than harmony at the auction: he would pit Highlanders against Sepiks, Catholics against Protestants. Thus, he surreptitiously attached a package of condoms to the picture frames donated by the local pharmacist and insisted that the Catholics present (who included a priest and several nuns) could *not* abstain from bidding on these items. Another of his more dangerous jokes involved a case of Mobil engine oil. After warning the hotel's manager and cook that this was not for frying chips, he solicited a bid from a former pilot – a man whose Mobil-lubricated engine had suffered catastrophic failure – saying that if he were still flying, this item would be of interest to him.

Such comments had their intended effect: they did indeed create an atmosphere of convivial competition. Bidding was reasonably animated on what was, in fact, a fairly wide assortment of goods and services. For instance, a Honda water pump (donated by the Papua New Guinean manager of Toba Motors) went for K510; and a ten-minute helicopter trip over Wewak (donated by the European pilot for Helipacific) went for K110.

The big spender of the evening was the Papua New Guinean manager of Wewak's Mobil Oil depot and service station. He and his wife had also won the prize for the best-dressed couple, a dinner for two donated by the Papua New Guinean owner of a local hotel. He bought the following: a case of Pepsi Cola donated by the Papua New Guinean owner of a local retail trade store; a case of Coca Cola donated by the company's European trade representative; a portable radio cassette unit donated by the Chinese owner of a local retail and wholesale store; an "executive" briefcase, raincoat, T-shirt and cap donated by the Papua New Guinean business manager of one of the country's English-language daily newspapers; a set of sports equipment, including a soccer ball and a rugby ball, donated by the European trade representatives of Puma Sports and Supervalue Wholesale Distributors; and a circular saw donated by the Papua New Guinean manager of the local branch of Steamships Hardware. He spent, in all, K735 – and went home, he told us, very pleased with the evening. This was so not only because he had acquired useful items, but also because the items he had donated (two cases of aforementioned motor oil and a fountain pen set) went for good prices (K90 and K95, respectively).

Others also bid generously: a European parish priest spent K525; the European owner of an oil-tank construction firm (which had recently completed a facility at a massive, internationally financed gold mine, soon to open on Lihir Island) spent K340; the Papua New Guinean headmaster of Wewak's International School spent K210

The final tabulations were made and the books closed on the auction a few days later at the club's next regular meeting. According to information distributed, those attending had spent K5,280 on the auction and K2,563.30 on the dinner, a raffle, several other fund-raising diversions and on various special items such as paintings donated by students at a local teacher's college. After expenses (principally the cost of the meal), the Rotary Club netted K5,980.82. Members reflected on the event with considerable satisfaction. They were pleased not only with the amount raised, which would allow them to finance a number of service projects, but also with the way it had been raised. The evening was a success. It was regarded as more than a means to an end. It was an end in itself.

For the duration of its annual dinner-auction, the Rotary Club of Wewak had coalesced Wewak's middle class into a momentarily complete, organically solidary community based upon an apparently seamless union of self *and* service. And as self and service became linked in an immediate and ostensible manner, the connection between private interest and public interest became more than just an article of capitalist faith in an hypothesized long-term (see Parry, 1989). Indeed, the dinner-auction became a virtual *tour de force* of capitalist adjustment and justification: it was an occasion to portray, and exuberantly enact, as noncontradictory a set of linked distinctions central to modernist social and economic interaction and obligation. In so doing, gifts and commodities, cooperation and competition, social entailment and disentailment could no longer be as readily – or as necessarily – seen to be disjunctive.[15] In what approached the best of all possible worlds, donors from a wide range of commercial specialties received favorable publicity, and hence future business reward,[16] for their gifts of commodities; bidders from a range of professional and business occupations competed jovially for good buys in an exemplary free and fair market (in the auction, participation was open to all present and value was transparently determined);[17] monies raised were to be used as gifts – to the excluded but still deserving less-fortunate. By what was, in effect, a muddling or at least partial collapse of these distinctions increasingly pervading everyday Papua New Guinea life, the Wewak Rotary Club provided a template for the formation of a middle-class sociality: it was a sociality of the unentailed but voluntarily concerned. It was a sociality of neighbors, not of kin.

For the nationals, who were among an emergent middle class, the template authorized what was for many a hard and painful transition in lifestyle. As middle-class consumers, if not entrepreneurs, entailed commitments of kinship or gift exchange were almost impossible to maintain in a commodity economy. The dinner-auction facilitated a reconfiguration, both in ideology and in action, of such particularist and enduring ties into a diffuse middle-class sociality.[18] For the expats, in effect direct heirs of Paul Harris, the template did not have to assist them to break ties and reorient relationships, Rather, it worked to affirm the rightness of a way of life long underway by promising that the alienation and social discord of a striving capitalist individualism were not inevitable.[19]

It must be stressed that the dinner-auction was not just an occasion for individuals of certain identities and interests to engage amicably in diffuse sociality. It was, as well, an occasion for these individuals to exhibit a heightened collective consciousness of their membership in a special kind of social category. Selected by Rotarians from the community at large as suitable, they acceded to – indeed, by all evidence, embraced – an ambience that invoked a moral community. In part, this community became defined, bounded and solidified through the operation of the dangerous humor. This humor evoked certain widely recognized tensions – those arising from commercial, ethnic, and religious competition as well as from personal delicts and difficulties – only to treat them all as amusingly idiosyncratic.[20] Certainly, this humor defined those present as sufficiently solidary that they could tease each other without taking offense.[21] At the same time, such humor provided public recognition that those present knew a lot about each other and, therefore, were bound together, not only in mutual tolerance, but in mutual regulation. Thus, Wewak Rotarians provided an annual context in which they and like-minded others could make manifest with minimized ambivalence and awareness of contradiction that they composed a class with acknowledged interests.

Conclusion

We have discussed a moment in the complex process of class happenings, a process, as mentioned, more historically than ethnographically documented. We have provided a relatively thick description of the way a group of relatively affluent Papua New Guineans has been gaining a new kind of consciousness about differences and similarities – about identities and interests – through engaging in the Rotary Club of Wewak, either as club members or as participants in club activities. Their engagement, although clearly not the sole cause of their new consciousness, played, we think, an important role in actualizing and manifesting the modernist transformations underway in Papua New Guinea. Indeed, they would fully agree that, in accord with the Rotary template, they had an important role in (to reiterate) "energizing and transforming civil society" (Hooper, n.d.: 22).

Yet, however optimistic and energetic members of this class might be, they – and their expat associates – were, after all, confronting a world affected by the increasing power of corporate and multinational capitalism, a fact to which we will briefly return in our conclusion, where we consider the long-term implications of the Rotary and the other templates we will discuss for an emerging Papua New Guinean middle class. In our next chapter, we describe another set of contexts and engagements for forging the redefinitions central to class happenings: whereas the Rotary allowed the affluent to emerge as the middle class, an organization of middle-class businesswomen redefined the grass roots as the lower class.

2
How the grass roots became the poor

The sleights of hand in the construction of desire

We have been documenting a locally acknowledged shift in the nature of inequality in Papua New Guinea whereby differences in life's circumstances and prospects were increasingly shifting from degree to kind, from commensurate to incommensurate. In the last chapter we saw members of the middle class defining themselves as "chiefs" relative to their grass-roots kin and, thereby, as ontological superiors. In their turn, members of the grass roots, recognizing structural exclusion, were becoming angry. They were afraid that they or their children (as, for instance, children who wanted Western-style education but had failed their exams or could not afford the costs) were no longer in the game, no longer even potential contenders.[1] Indeed, they often spoke of their "jealousy" and their desire to "bring down" to their level those who, in an increasingly unfair system, had been able to acquire significantly more than they (Gewertz and Errington, 1991a).

At the same time, many of these same grass-roots Papua New Guineans, righteously angry about developing class differences, would also acknowledge – sometimes ruefully, sometimes resentfully – that they and their occasional meager accumulations were also frequently the subject of jealousy and subsequent leveling demands. Even those who resided in rural villages or in urban squatter settlements often remarked how difficult it was to fulfill kin (and linked ritual) obligations in an increasingly cash-based world[2] – how hard it was to save money for such virtual necessities as clothing and school fees, to say nothing of saving for such "goods" as radio cassette-players.

In this chapter, we describe certain processes at work to deflect this anger, jealousy and resentment – on the one hand, between the grass roots and the emerging elite, and on the other hand, among the grass roots – in such a way that individual accumulation came to appear not only practically feasible but also morally justified. These processes, reflecting middle-class expectations, were based on a modernist claim that almost everyone could gain access to a certain quality of life. Almost everyone had the *potential* opportunity and capacity – indeed the right and virtual obligation – to work and to save so as to consume self-evidently desirable goods and services.[3]

Correspondingly, according to this formulation, those unable or unwilling to accumulate and thereby acquire these goods and services would have primarily themselves to blame. Any ensuing – and persisting – inequality would thus be understood as less the product of unfair exclusion or repudiation of kin obligations than of personal failure to fulfill reasonable expectations. (We discuss the redefinition of reasonability according to middle-class standards at greater length in chapters 5 and 6.) Indeed, such a perspective, focusing on personal responsibility for failure in (what was being defined as) an open and just system, undercut the idea that categorical exclusion was even a systemic possibility. Thus, in a modernist *faux*-revival of egalitarianism, differences would appear, once again, to be based on degree and not kind – they would appear to reflect a relatively fluid continuum of personal attributes rather than a relatively closed set of categorical differences. Hence, through the virtual sleights of hand, what were – and we strongly suspected would remain – the slights of class exclusion were being presented as reflecting less social injustice than individual failure.

Our ethnographic focus here is on Sepik Women in Trade (called SWIT by its members), a private organization begun by middle-class women in Wewak during our 1996 field research. SWIT's explicit objective was to assist impoverished women living primarily in Wewak's squatter settlements to market their handicrafts – their baskets, string bags, clay pots and shell and bead jewelry. This ensuing income would help them meet their families' basic subsistence needs, including school fees. Significantly in the course of weekly meetings, SWIT's initial focus shifted from exploring ways to assist women struggling to make ends meet to exhorting them to work harder and save more so as to attend an international trade fair in Jayapura, Indonesia. Attending this trade fair was presented as a great opportunity: not only would it be enjoyable, but it would facilitate establishing lucrative markets, and would ensure future prosperity. Indeed, many of the hard-pressed women who became active in SWIT because they recognized themselves in the organization's rhetoric – as "the poor women sitting long hours at the market or by the side of the road waiting to sell their handicrafts" – came strongly to believe that going to Jayapura was both highly desirable and an eminently reasonable expectation. Conversely, to miss this business opportunity came to suggest that their poverty was deserved.

To understand this transformation and its systemic effects, we explore how people, in an effort to maintain the relative equality of commensurate (rather than incommensurate) differences, came to accept the (supposed) justice of the capitalist market. Crucially, although this market was described in SWIT's rhetoric both as requiring self-regimentation and as providing vast (hitherto unimagined) opportunities for self-augmentation, it was said to enhance rather than decrease social equality. SWIT's rhetoric, thus, was an effort to present capitalism in a way that would enhance rather than detract from the lives of Papua New Guinea's grass roots.

The beginnings of SWIT

We, like most of the fifty or so women who initially responded, became aware of SWIT and its first public meeting from notices taped to the door of the Wewak post office and displayed at various churches. According to the notices, the meeting was called by the provincial government's Department of Commerce and Industry; its purpose was to help women by promoting the sale of their handicrafts. During the five months that Deborah attended weekly meetings, participation grew to include some 200 women, many of whom we spoke to concerning their interest in the group and their life circumstances more generally.

SWIT's first public meeting followed almost a year of planning.[4] It was convened by a number of tertiary-educated, relatively affluent, English-speaking women, who had frequently met during 1995 to discuss the need for such a group. These included the owner of a local dress shop, the owner of a tourist guest house, the owner of a small betel nut plantation as well as the Director of the Department of Commerce and Industry, the owner of a nursery providing potted plants for interior decoration, and a staff member at a nongovernmentally funded women's organization. According to the minutes of these early meetings and the "information paper" eventually submitted to the Provincial Executive Council, these "leading business women" wished to promote market opportunities at home and abroad. In addition, as part of their "initiative," they wished to "assist grass-roots women to promote and advance their creativity skills" and to "strengthen and maintain Sepik's traditional designs and art work" (PEC Information Paper, 8 November 1995: 1–2).

The first and subsequent meetings began (and ended) with a prayer. At the first meeting, the chairwoman (the owner of the dress shop) explained that SWIT's project was a Christian one, to help Wewak's "less fortunate" women. It had several dimensions. As "an organization to help local producers," SWIT would provide Sepik women with a guaranteed market. It would buy their handicrafts and resell them to national and international markets, for example, to hotels, museums and artifact shops. For this to be possible, anyone who wished to join SWIT and have her handicrafts bought by the organization must pay a K25 yearly membership fee. This would provide operating money prior to receipt of resale revenues. SWIT would, as well, buy and resell the materials from which the handicrafts were made: the grass for the baskets, the bark for the string bags, the shells and beads for the jewelry. In addition to selling items at a central location in Wewak, SWIT would actively seek out national and international markets. Several of these had already been located, as would be explained at future meetings. Finally, SWIT would help women attend international trade fairs. Women made many beautiful and useful things yet only men went to the fairs to sell their artifacts. That should be changed.

After SWIT's essential mission was explained, representatives were selected from Wewak's nineteen major church groups. These representatives were emissaries to introduce SWIT to their social circles. The selection of church groups was altogether consistent with the organization's Christian ethos as evidenced by the invocation of God's assistance, the concern in helping the less fortunate, and, as we shall see, in the use of often explicit Christian rhetoric.

The meeting was then opened for discussion. A woman from one of Wewak's squatter settlements, though clearly moved by SWIT's vision, had an important question:

> Women's work has always been hard. Up until this point no one has considered it. No one has helped us plan and develop so that we might be able to earn money to help our families. The government has ignored us. At last this road has opened so that each woman can spend money

> [on the SWIT membership fee] – yes – but that money will help her find markets to earn more money to bring back to her house. I want to thank God for letting . . . [the organizers] open this road for us. Sepik baskets and bilums have a particular look. I am from Yangaru and am sorry when I see people from there wear Highland's bilums. I take this as my challenge to promote Yangaru bilums. I also take it as my challenge to open people's eyes as to what Sepik women make. No one knows our work. When there are fairs, it is always men who go. We don't know why – maybe to find other women. We will succeed because we are challenged. We work hard in our houses and make beautiful things but it is always our men and our children who have the "numbers" [recognition]. Let us pray for those here who are leading us. They are working for us. They have their own families but are taking the time to help us.
>
> But I do have one question. Why can't groups join SWIT so that women can pool their money together? K25 is a lot.

Her question focused directly on what came to be a major and continuing theme of SWIT meetings: why could kinswomen not help each other with membership fees and benefit as a group? SWIT leaders, however, remained adamant that "businesswomen" must be personally responsible for their economic failures and successes. If others were to have access to their businesses as shareholders or as claimants, the businesses would likely fail. SWIT's leadership (and undoubtedly most national Rotarians) could testify to this from their own struggles to create – and protect – successful businesses. (Indeed, as the chairwoman later told us, she had failed several times when in business with her husband because he was ruinously generous to their kin. However, her present business under her sole control was doing well. She stressed that she felt largely absolved from future kin claims, especially since these kin, who had been happy to take her money, had not helped her when her businesses were in trouble.)

Moreover, SWIT's leaders continued, if several women did join together to buy a single membership, further problems would ensue. Jealousies would break out when, for instance, one worked harder than the others and, as well, when funds would allow only one to go to a trade fair. And money earned from the sale of handicrafts would have to be divided and thus no one would earn very much. Also, no one would earn very much if a member allowed herself to be talked into selling for another: in such a case, she would "only be cheating herself."

Although one could imagine ways to deal with all of these

potential problems, the association of good business practices – that which would result in enhanced income and status (as a leading businesswoman who had a "number") – and individual responsibility became the unchallengeable (at least in public) premise of the group. Although SWIT leaders recognized a commonality among poor women who lacked business opportunities, they always defined SWIT as constituted on behalf of individuals: it was (like urban religious affiliation[5]) to be a freely entered into association benefiting unrelated women who had joined together out of generalizable self-interest. Accordingly, SWIT's dominant discourse soon featured as its dominant theme the right and responsibility of an *individual* woman to work sufficiently hard to attend the forthcoming trade fair in Jayapura, where her handicrafts could be seen and purchased by international buyers. This trip was repeatedly described as a great opportunity; conversely, if missed, a woman had only herself to blame, since she had over five months to save up for it.

The sale of handicrafts, particularly brightly colored baskets, had long been important to the several hundred Chambri women who, in 1996, lived in Chambri Camp, the largest single-ethnic squatter settlement in Wewak. (We, too, in our many years of work with Chambri had lived in this squatter settlement.) Indeed, the economic viability of their families largely depended upon basket sales, which brought more money to the camp than any other activity. Although a few squatters had jobs with fortnightly salaries or received remittances from those elsewhere who did have salaries, and some earned money selling black-market beer, the vast majority depended on the sale of handicrafts to get by. And they did get by, but just. In fact, if Chambri settlement women did not make baskets, they probably would not themselves have been able to use them: few could afford the K15 that such a relative luxury would cost.

Life for most of these women involved a routine of drying the basket reeds sent from Chambri Lake (where they grew up in profusion during the dry season), of dyeing them with store-bought pigments in large tins of water placed to boil upon open fires, and of weaving them into baskets of various sizes and shapes. Women frequently shared their reeds and dyes with sisters and other kinswomen living in the camp. But it was in the weaving where a community of women truly took shape: affines and agnates sat for long hours on mats, legs stretched out in front of them, as they deftly turned their reeds into baskets. They chatted about life in the camp, about news from home and about innovations they planned for their

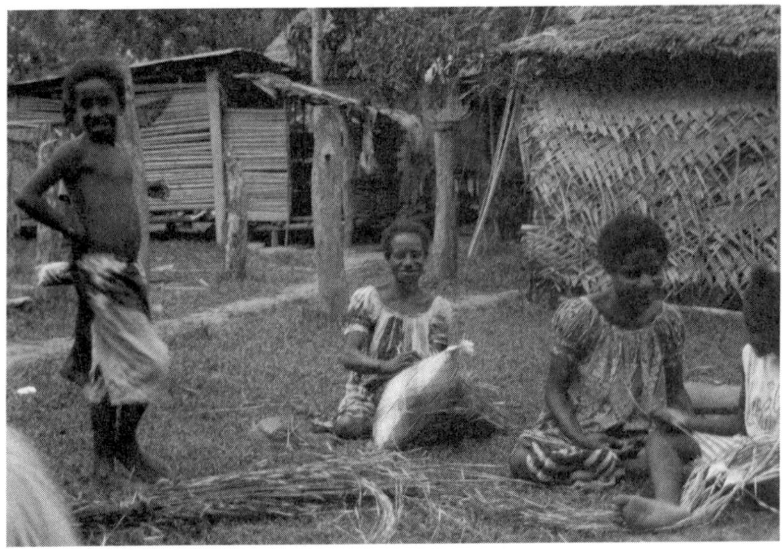

4. It was in weaving baskets that a community of Chambri women truly took place.

work. The innovation might be a heart-shaped basket or perhaps a backpack.

Interestingly, most of the women knew little or nothing about the historical precedent to their activity. These same reeds had been woven by Chambri women into mosquito bags – called *arenk* – and traded throughout the Middle Sepik region before they were replaced by the mosquito nets introduced by Europeans. Many of these women had been born in Wewak; several had never visited their home villages; a few spoke a little of the Chambri language. Consequently, lots had never even heard the term *arenk*. Among those who had heard the term, or had been told about these mosquito bags, only one or two had ever seen one. Yet they all claimed basket-weaving as a quintessentially Chambri activity and objected vociferously and ethnocentrically to those Sepik upstarts (and children of dogs) who had stolen the monopoly which was rightly theirs. They were fortunate, they said, that their settlement fronted the main road from the airport. Thus, the two stands constructed to display Chambri handicrafts were more accessible than those built by these other Sepiks. (Both stands were shared with men who exhibited carved masks and spears. One was constructed and used by Chambri from the home villages of Indingai and

Wombun, the other, by Chambri from Kilimbit.) A buyer sufficiently affluent to acquire such items could just pull up in a car (itself a mark of considerable affluence) to make a purchase – and there would always be several women around to take the money, not only for themselves but for others.

However, this money if more than a few kina, as with all money known or thought to be entering the camp, would become immediately subject to redistribution, as kin and others would ask to borrow money or be compensated for past injury or repaid for past help. And while it must be noted that Chambri enjoyed being able to redistribute to their kin, they also found it very hard to do so when the portion they could reserve for themselves dwindled to virtually nothing.

It was from these women, then, whose production and revenues were embedded in networks of support, sociability and entailment, that SWIT was drawing its prospective entrepreneurs. It was these who were to work hard and save so as to further their individual self-interests by attending the Jayapura trade fair with other, like-minded, nascent businesswomen.

Jayapura: the normalization of desire

The weekly SWIT meetings followed a standard format. Framed (as we have said) by prayers, they also included reading, discussing and approving the minutes as well as considering new business. In part because the early minutes focused on the creation of SWIT, deliberation about them provided a context for women to express lingering concerns about the conditions of membership. Women still balked at the amount of the annual K25 fee and at the necessity of single rather than group membership. However, SWIT's leaders remained adamant. Indeed, they augmented their argument by insisting that fostering individual enterprise was not only inherently desirable but accorded with recent shifts in governmental policy. This policy (partially driven by the previously discussed "structural adjustments" imposed by the World Bank and the International Monetary Fund) was designed to wean Papua New Guineans away from reliance on "handouts." Such a reliance on handouts, or an expectation of "something for nothing," was, they insisted, generally understood as responsible for a multitude of widely recognized Papua New Guinea ills: economic stagnation, corruption and general moral decline (especially of the youth). In this regard, it was made clear that the help offered by the Commerce and Industry Department would be limited to business advice and display space and that its role would be to help SWIT members help themselves.[6]

Women also inquired during these early discussions of the minutes, whether they could continue to attend meetings without joining. They wished to see if SWIT proved sufficiently successful to be worth their K25. In particular, they wondered when it would start buying things from them. Leaders responded by reminding these women that SWIT could only begin buying when it had accrued sufficient funds through membership fees. Moreover, SWIT could only display what had been purchased once the Commerce and Industry Department, convinced of SWIT's success, provided space. Thus, SWIT could only wait for a limited time and would have to implement a cut-off date after which they could not join. In addition, a cut-off date was necessary since the Jayapura trade fair was approaching and leaders had to know who and how many would be attending.

Significantly, by the third meeting, arrangements to go to this trade fair were becoming the primary agenda item. As such, these arrangements came to be the focus of subsequent minutes – and the discussion of the minutes. Consequently, the concerns about conditions of membership which were, in fact, ongoing, had little opportunity to be formally addressed. Moreover, these concerns – the exigencies of the mundane present – were increasingly dispelled as women – members and leaders alike – became increasingly dazzled by the vivid elaborations of the brave new world that could be theirs through the trip to Jayapura.

Not only would the trip be an exceptional business opportunity for women to probe international markets by showing their handicrafts; it would also be a wonderful excursion – entertaining as well as educational – especially for the majority of the members who had traveled little, much less outside of the country. (It would have been, thus, much like the trip to Calgary for Rotarians.) SWIT members would be outfitted in what had become the traditional uniforms of modernist Papua New Guinea: *meri* blouses and *laplaps* (voluminous blouses and wrap-around skirts, introduced by missionaries) in the yellow, red and black of the Papua New Guinea flag (to be purchased at K30 per outfit, or made for oneself). They would travel in a group by air and stay at several guest houses. SWIT leaders had negotiated special rates with Air Niugini (K350 per round-trip ticket) and guest house managers (K15 per person, per night). Women could cook in their accommodations. However, they might decide to try local foods: these were delicious and just like those found in Papua New Guinea, but prepared very differently – with lots of hot spices. Although it was, in fact, possible to cut costs by, for example, going overland and by boat, it would be far better if SWIT members traveled together as a delegation – as "ambassadors" representing their country in a foreign one. And this foreign country, in contrast to their own, was one in which "security was tight": police had a great deal of power and were very efficient. Consequently, because there was little criminal activity, women could feel safe. Indeed, if it were not for a relative absence of religious freedom, life in Jayapura would be much better than life in Wewak, particularly for business-persons who would not have to worry about break-ins and other robberies. (We explore this concern with law and order among members of the middle class in considerable detail in chapter 5.) As safe as it was, children should not be taken since the women would be very busy selling their handicrafts and performing "traditional" Sepik songs and dances at the fair. Therefore, the women should make certain that someone would look out for their children during the eight days of the trip. It would be exciting to be away from families. There was, of course, the problem of getting permission from husbands. As regrettable as this might be, it would be foolish for someone to go or attempt to go without her husband's permission. Women should, therefore, start early to broach the subject to husbands, explaining what a great opportunity the trip would be and one that would ultimately benefit the entire family.

To be sure, some women did wonder aloud whether the practical difficulties of making the trip – however appealing – would be limited to getting husbands and families lined up. One, clearly affluent woman asked for a "detailed budget," saying that as far as she could see the trip "will be at least K500 and not everyone can afford this." SWIT's president replied, reflecting (quite sincerely, we think) her sense of what it took to be a businesswoman: "This is your own initiative. There are no free handouts. If you have an interest in going, you will just have to work hard to get there. If inside your heart you want to go, and with God's help, then you will achieve your aim. You must budget your money. That way there will be fewer problems for everyone. We are not forcing you to go such that we have to pay your way."

Within the first few meetings of SWIT, going to Jayapura had become presented, thus, as an entirely reasonable and – for those who were properly motivated – achievable desire. "The poor women sitting long hours at the market or by the side of the road waiting to sell their handicrafts" had become national "ambassadors": from grass-roots women, whose difficulty in making ends meet was such that payment of the K25 SWIT membership was an acute hardship, they had been transformed into those whose major concerns were the essentially gendered – not specifically class-based – ones of arranging child-care and assuaging husbands.

SWIT's rhetoric, thus, substantially elided the facts of class (and gender) differences in Papua New Guinea such that the obviously desirable (epitomized by the trip to Jayapura) would be readily accessible to local women. No longer need any woman with initiative (and, one might add, the basic skills of domestic management) remain peripheral or excluded from the action.

In addition, SWIT's rhetoric soon came to suggest that the nature of and the reasons for existing structures of exclusion were themselves shifting. This was so whether exclusion stemmed from the peripherality of Papua New Guinea in general or from these women in particular. According to the revelation SWIT's president was shortly to present, in the near future one would not even have to travel to places like Jayapura to be connected to the wider world, though such trips might still be enjoyable and useful. Instead, the wider world was about to become entirely accessible on a daily basis. Her elaboration of what SWIT as an international marketing organization might offer was climaxed by an enthralling vision: it was not just about being a more effective operator in the mundane world, nor was it just about leaving the mundane world behind for the magic of Jayapura; it was about transforming that mundane world itself.

All that glitters

Before calling the 10 May meeting to order (SWIT's tenth), the president announced that, because the women present were interested in marketing, she had invited a special guest whom many probably already knew. He was the national director of Overseas Product Traders. After introducing himself as a former government patrol officer who, though from Madang, had worked in the Sepik for over thirty years, the director spoke for about forty minutes. Since retiring from the government service, he had done research in order to learn how he might best "help all the little people." And thus he came upon "network marketing." Using his own money, he had traveled to England to learn about Overseas Product Traders (OPT), a network marketing enterprise. Begun in 1989, OPT had become a worldwide operation which, through its collaboration with an organization called Australian Gold Bullion, was "like a bank investing in gold." Both individuals as well as groups could join OPT. He himself had become a member and had sponsored SWIT's president when she wished to join. She joined, as had he, by paying a K150 fee.

The director explained further by unrolling a chart entitled "Network Growth." This chart depicted a pyramid of boxes with sums next to each row. The first row of boxes represented those individuals one had sponsored: for each (who had paid the K150 fee), his or her sponsor got K20. The next row represented members signed up in their turn by those one had sponsored, along with the fee the immediate as well as apical sponsor received. This continued through four generations. Although the details of who got how much became very hard to follow, nonetheless the idea of one's initial investment and recruitment efforts paying off generously with little additional work was compellingly presented. Moreover, the money earned was invested by OPT, through Australian Gold Bullion, in the "safest investment there was" and one you could draw upon at any time.

At this point the director pulled from his attaché case a gold coin. "This could be yours," he said. "It is an ounce of gold worth 500 dollars. [Sharp intakes of breath from the audience.] Eventually [taking out a much larger coin] you could have this, a kilogram of gold worth 19,000 dollars – a primary product."

To a truly rapt audience, he continued:

> I am going to tell you now a story from my own life. I began to distrust paper money when Papua New Guinea devalued its currency [in 1994]. Then an old woman I know lost her entire savings when her house burned down. But my money in gold is safe: nothing can happen to it. When you join OPT you must sign a purchase agreement like this [pulling one from his attaché case] which will allow the company to buy and sell gold for you, at any time, at any place around the world. Then later you could, if you wanted to, become an international marketing associate at which point you must sign this form [taking out another one]. This is how it works. For K500 you buy units: 20 percent of your money goes into blue chip stocks which are the best; 20 percent into big

> projects like the [Papua New Guinea] Lihir gold mine or a South African gold mine; 20 percent of your money gets invested in banks; and 20 percent of your money is in a pool from which you can borrow. You get interest every day.
>
> Once you join, you have other benefits as well. I am at the moment finding markets for yams, taro, and sugar cane in Lae, Australia, and New Zealand. I have just come back from Port Moresby to work out the taxation, financing and contracts. And I am going to help women market string bags – I think there is a big market here. There are European, Australian, and American markets for string bags and also for coconut fiber brooms and grass baskets. People all over the world are recognizing the superiority of these products over whitemen's ones. . . .
>
> The United Nations knows about our company. And we are going to be on the Internet. It is one of my accomplishments to provide Papua New Guinea with a "trade point" on the Internet. I am working on getting Nestles to buy coffee and cacao and there are going to be markets for vanilla and seafoods. Sometimes I am asked whether the Papua New Guinea government knows about OPT. Let me tell you, both our government and the United Nations know about it. It is internationally recognized and operates in sixteen countries.[7]

In the question and answer session that followed, the principal and considerable interest was in OPT's plan to buy and sell yams and taro. The director elaborated in answer to the many inquiries of a highly responsive audience: though small yams would suffice for the Papua New Guinea trade, he would buy only big yams for overseas distribution, each at least 500 grams. And none should have holes because whitemen are afraid of insects. Concerning taro, he would buy only native taro, not the "Singapore" variety. He expected eventually to handle 5 tons a week. Although there were professors at universities trying to create better strains, he thought they were wasting their time because taro was already a salable product. He and OPT had confirmed the commercial viability of four already-common types. As he listed these types, the women became even more engaged – whispering to one another in recognition and assent. He would buy "big" taro, and apologized for knowing its name only in his native language, which he gave. He would buy the sticky white taro. And the yellow taro. And the pin-spotted taro. The women knew all of these types and began to call out their names in their different native languages. One woman then asked: "Will you be interested in the kinds of yams that have nails?" Yes, he would be. And he would eventually buy coconuts, sweet potatoes, sugar cane, and betel nut (but, remember, nothing with insects). When he told the women that they could make lots of money from selling betel nut because there were many uses for it, they beamed with pleasure. (It could be soaked and its extract put in toothpaste; what was left could be ground up and put in a tablet as a mild stimulant.)

After SWIT's president thanked him for coming, he promised that he would be seeking national and international markets in which to sell SWIT's handicrafts. He knew that it would be impossible for every member to spend K150 to join OPT, but perhaps the entire organization might be registered.

The director as well as the chairwoman and the other leaders of SWIT (all of whom we spoke to at length on occasions other than SWIT meetings) were sincerely engaged and excited about the ways in which the ordinary hardworking people – women in particular – could continue to do what they normally did, yet transform their lives by more effective marketing. They envisioned a just world in which virtually *any diligent Papua New Guinean exercising normal skills*, whether in weaving baskets or growing taro, would be well rewarded. This would be a world in which differential access to educational advantage no longer excluded most from the good life. This would be a world in which one did not have to be a Lihir Islander (literally, sitting on a gold mine) to benefit from the national and international economy. For example, with OPT and its linkage to Australian Gold Bullion, anyone could profit from the Lihir mine. This would be a world open to anyone alert to opportunity and willing to work hard. In this newly moral world, where *everyone* had ready access to ample opportunities, one could with equanimity attend to one's own interests without being continually wrenched by the claims of kin for financial help. Such claims, if still encountered, could be charitably dismissed as both illegitimate and as fostering a disabling dependency – a handout mentality. One might, of course, choose to live among one's kin – much as the chairwoman did in one of Wewak's squatter settlements. But life would be different as people got their priorities straight: as they worked hard and saved their money (so as, for example, to convert their houses from bush to permanent materials – again, as the chairwoman was doing – and, perhaps, put in electricity). And one might, as indeed one should, still engage in initiatives to help the less fortunate. But this would be freely given (Christian) charity. Neither a world of unfair, arbitrary, and categorical exclusions (of incommensurate differences), nor of initiative-stifling redistribution (nor, one might add, of dog-eat-dog capitalist competition), it would be one in which Papua New Guineans, whoever they were and wherever they lived, could, *if they made the right choices*, lead lives of industry and comfort. Put another way, they could lead lives of prosperous, disciplined Christian equality.[8]

It would thus be, in effect, as the vanguard of a prospective Papua New Guinea *petit bourgeois* revolution that SWIT's ambassadors would enter Jayapura to claim their rightful place in the global economy.

The slights of hand in the construction of desire

The women who continued to attend weekly SWIT meetings were presented with a beguiling vision of a transformed future – with a vision evoking something of a reversed "cargoism." Unlike those "natives" who had sought a transformed future premised on (among other things) the conviction that their own indigenous goods were vastly less desirable than imported, manufactured ones and unlike those who had sought a restored past premised on the conviction that their old ways were, after all, *their* ways, these women were encouraged to believe that their traditional skills and products were fully modern and fully marketable.[9] Because, for example, their indigenous coconutfiber brooms were highly valued on an international market (as attested to by the United Nations and as soon to be advertised on the Internet), they could pick and choose in a postcolonial world to which they were fully connected. This was a world that had at last gone their way.[10]

As it turned out, eighty-eight SWIT women (including sixteen government employees) – about 40 percent of those who initially had signed up to go – attended the Jayapura trade fair. (Because we left the field before the trip, our evidence here is based on correspondence with the chairwoman and others and on a summary report submitted to the provincial government ["Participation at 1996 Jayapura Expo," 1996].) Though many traveled by the tiring but less expensive sea and land routes and some found the food too spicy, all enjoyed the trip. Yet, none covered her costs. As the summary report to the provincial government stated:

> For the first three (3) nights, most of the items were not sold out due to pricing. Most items were priced according to PNG rate, which was too high for Indonesians. However, the women lowered their prices and sold

> out their items towards the end of the event . . . [Moreover] nothing was for nothing. Women had to make numerous financial contributions towards the services provided by interpreters, escorts and bus drivers. These caused a lot of inconveniences to their budget after meeting airfares and other travel expenses. (5, 7)

Nonetheless, the trip was experienced not only as pleasurable but as auspicious since it provided an opportunity to learn "the language of trade" – the terms and concepts of international marketing.

So impressed did the chairwoman, herself, remain with the prospects of international marketing, in part confirmed by the Jayapura trip, that she planned to purchase a laptop (as advocated and marketed by OPT) so as to be among the first in Wewak to monitor prospects – "find markets" – on the Internet. Given the cost of the laptop – certainly in excess of K2,000 – and the current unavailability of phone lines in Wewak suitable for Internet access, the chairwoman was certainly exhibiting a robust confidence in the future.

Of the eight Chambri women who had signed up for the Jayapura trip, only three actually went: a nurse who lived in housing provided for her at Wewak's hospital; her sister, who lived at Chambri Camp and ran a black-market beer business; and the wife of a schoolteacher who with her husband had (like the chairwoman) nearly completed a permanent-materials house at Chambri Camp. Although all three women did weave and sell baskets, none was a poor mother dependent on the sale of her handicrafts. In fact, none of the grass-roots Chambri women who had been targeted by SWIT "to promote and advance their creativity skills" could afford to attend. While we do know they were disappointed and frustrated because they could not manage to go, we can only speculate (at this point in our research) as to whether they blamed themselves for their inadequacy. Certainly, to repeat, the entire logic of SWIT and the recurrent theme of its rhetoric was to effect a sleight of hand whereby poor women *who continued to sit* by the side of the road or the market would become transformed from the less fortunate into those responsible for their own failures.

Conclusion: learning capitalist culture in a Papua New Guinean modernity

We have here described a shift in the nature of inequality from differences based upon degree to differences based upon kind – from differences, relatively transitory, to differences, relatively fixed.

Organizations like SWIT have contributed to this shift by neutralizing and deflecting righteous indignation concerning socio-economic exclusion. SWIT has done so by defining the pursuit and attainment of a middle-class lifestyle not only as inherently good – both materially and morally – but as inherently available. It thus presented such a lifestyle in egalitarian terms, as within the reach of everyone sufficiently productive and disciplined to work hard to supply what the global economy demanded and to resist dependency-perpetuating claims from less enterprising kin and others.

Like Rotary, SWIT defined what it meant to be a member of the middle class. But SWIT also simultaneously constructed and justified the existence of a lower class. Through SWIT's construction of the world, being poor – or at least remaining poor – became a matter of choice, not of inescapable circumstance. In effect, SWIT served to redefine the broad category of grass-roots women into those who were deserving and those who were not. Poverty (at least as it was continuing rather than temporary) hence became not simply an overwhelmingly difficult and unfair life circumstance with which most women must somehow cope; it became a matter of degree directly reflective of personal character and worth. In effect, SWIT promulgated at least a variant of a capitalist ideology which held that "inequalities of income and wealth [were fair because they] measure[d], however roughly, the economic contributions of men and women who embark[ed] their energies and resources in the productive process" (Lekachman, 1977: 107). This particular capitalist doctrine of social justice, as disseminated and given a Christian inflection by Wewak's "leading businesswomen," created a lower-class "other" whose anger about developing class inequalities became neutralized into petty (and thereby easily dismissed) complaints about the lack of "free handouts." Conversely, given the presentations of Jayapura and OPT as undeniably alluring and evidently accessible, it was not easy for those who remained stuck at home (without Gold Bullion) to evade a certain definition of themselves. By wasting their God-given talents and the opportunity provided them by SWIT's community-minded Christian businesswomen, they had only themselves to blame for remaining poor women without prospects.

That SWIT members were receiving a sentimental education in self-blame did not, of course, mean that they fully accepted the lessons presented to them at their weekly meetings. Although some SWIT members were clearly let down and embarrassed when they could not make the deposit necessary for the Jayapura trip, we do not doubt that they, and others, might nonetheless think their way out of SWIT's particular rhetorical snares such that they would still feel unfairly disadvantaged in an increasingly inequitable system. We also have little doubt that the dominant discourse of SWIT (and comparable organizations) was undermining the political legitimacy of oppositional thought and sociality. In the next chapter, we explore this undermining – to the point of political impotence – in more detail.

3
The realization of class exclusions

Golf and the redrawing of boundaries of sociality

In the last two chapters, we showed that the consumption-oriented sociality through which relatively affluent Papua New Guineans were defining their identities and interests was importantly realized in contexts of mostly imported activities and organizations. Rotary provided one such context. SWIT, substantially through its affiliation with OPT, provided another. In particular, we saw that membership in both Rotary and SWIT furnished those of the middle class with their justification for seeking a good life in which they could, with equanimity, attend to their own affairs without being continually wrenched by the claims of grass-roots kin for financial help. Golf provided a third such context of sociality. It was at the Wewak Resort and Country Club where we found clearly instantiated and recognized a key constellation of the processes constituting middle-class life worldwide: commodity consumption by individuals within nuclear (or, at the broadest, nucleated) families. And it was around the margins of this context of sociality provided by Wewak's golf club that we found this constellation to be especially clearly, if unsuccessfully, challenged.

Preliminaries: on golf and the good life

An active, almost evangelical, promotion of these worldwide processes constituting middle-class life (those that were coming Wewak's way at the margins of the "developing" world) came our way (at the center of "development") in a recent *New York Times* article (Sandomir, 1997: D1 and 8). This was about Tiger Woods, 21-year-old golfer *extraordinaire*. Not only was Woods a thoroughly multicultural hero (self-designated as "Cablinasian" – part Caucasian, Black, American Indian, Chinese and Thai),[1] but he owed much of his success as a golfer to direct and positive parental influence. Woods' father, in particular, had focused much of his life on him, to ensure that he developed the discipline and skills necessary for success. Significantly, the two remained very close, with Woods' father continuing as active advisor and coach.

According to this article, Woods had agreed to serve as an American Express spokesman during the next five years. The multimillion dollar deal was described as an American Express "coup" over competing credit card companies – a coup which might, for instance, "crimp Mastercard's efforts to further market and promote its golf sponsorship interests" (D8). Speaking with satisfaction about the agreement, the president of American Express stated that Tiger Woods' traits of "'discipline, hard-work, and preparation are the pillars of our business'" (D1, 8). Other analysts of the credit card industry were cited: they described Woods as a valuable addition to the American Express promotional line-up. "'It's hard to visualize anyone he wouldn't appeal to'" (D8), said one. Another characterized him as a "global personality who could be used to market American Express's products in South America and Asia, where growth exists in golf and credit cards" (D8). For his part, Woods said that this contract was in accord with what he and his advisors "'had already developed [as] a brand plan that encompasses who I am'" (D8). He also said he was "touched" that American Express was donating $1 million to his charitable foundation, "to benefit junior golf for minorities" (D1).

Tiger Woods, as global agent for American Express, was, in short, an upstanding young man (the product of strong parental influence) who, in his multiculturalism and his golf – and his AMEX card (that you don't want to leave home without) – would be "accepted" virtually anywhere. He embodied a global – and globalizing – vision of a world that rewarded individualistic striving. According to this vision, perhaps even minorities (and their youths) could play the game, given a proper role model and an occasional helping hand.

By chance, but not entirely coincidentally, the day after the *New York Times* article appeared, National Public Radio (21 May 1997) broadcast in its evening news a piece about consumer credit card borrowing. (After all, lenders such as American Express were often newsworthy because of their importance to the United States' economy: American Express's 19.6 percent of the market share of credit card purchases was $129.6 billion annually [Sandomir, 1997: D8].) According to the speaker, the majority of Americans not only had little retirement savings but were borrowed up to their credit card limits, barely able to pay the high interest rates, much less pay off the debt.

On yet the following day, we ourselves received an instructive but, again, not entirely surprising advertisement from one of our Visa Card companies. (Visa was the leader in the credit card market, with $308.7 billion in annual spending for a 46.6 percent market share [D8].) In ways that seamlessly conflated needs, wants and goods, we were asked: "Why put off buying the things you need now when your new lower rate [15.4 percent] makes it all so affordable" (Gooden, 1997). In particular, it was suggested that we might want to upgrade our old computer and/or take the vacation we had been putting off until we had saved some extra cash. Significantly, such purchases, at this lower interest rate, were also to be understood as "rewards" for our having managed finances "responsibly" (Gooden, 1997).

To sum up, Tiger Woods had become an embodiment and global emissary – an encapsulating symbol – for a complex of socio-economic phenomena: for the worldwide penetration of certain forces and forms of modern capital whereby proper socialization, display, consumption and responsibility were linked. Conversely, his example implied that those unable to display and consume were the poorly socialized and irresponsible. Although Papua New Guinea was not yet South America and Asia, the hot areas for growth in both golf and credit cards targeted by American Express, Woods' message would find an increasingly receptive audience there.[2]

The Wewak Resort and Country Club: sketches of place and participants

Among those particularly receptive to the message Woods had come to embody would be the sixty paid-up members and their families of the Wewak Resort and Country Club, known generally as the golf club. Three-quarters of these were nationals. Each had paid the annual membership fee of K200, with a few wives paying an additional K25 for "associate" membership. In addition, greens fees were K6 per game. Although these fees were low in comparison to those charged in Port Moresby (where the annual membership fee, we were told, was K1,000 and where, even so, the club was usually fully enrolled), very few in Wewak could afford to pay them and the other attendant expenses of golf, such as clubs, balls and caddies.

The elite status of Wewak's golfers was evident to all, in part given the public location of this private club and course: it was situated a few miles outside Wewak, along a major road leading to a prison, a high school and a number of squatter settlements and villages. Hundreds, if not thousands, passed the imposing clubhouse and well-manicured grounds each day. Some, the relatively affluent, were in cars, but most were packed into buses or trucks, or were on foot. The golfers came to the club in cars.

The others coming to the club were largely women and children who walked from the nearby squatter settlements. They sat – in a spatial encoding of class differences – on the margin, under the trees adjacent to the parking lot. The boys hoped to earn a bit of money as caddies (and, when no one was around, by finding balls to sell back); the women and girls hoped to earn a bit as providers of snacks (oranges, popcorn, coconuts), or sometimes as providers of whole dinners to golfing families going home; the few men just chatted, smoked, chewed betel nut, and watched the golfers. Some of these men told us that they had learned the game by watching and thought they could be good at it. One, our Chambri friend Michael Kamban, was, as we will later discuss in more detail, waiting to waylay his national parliamentary representative who was sure to visit the golf club when in town.

As we inquired into the history of the course, we were directed by virtually everyone to an expat who was a long-time golfer and club member. This man had been a crocodile-skin and artifact buyer, but was currently manager of a fuel depot. Very willing to speak about the history of the course, he told us that it was unusual (if not unique) in Papua New Guinea, because it had been constructed to serve the golfing interests of an indigenous elite, steadily growing in number. This was some ten years after Independence, at a time when expats – whose jobs were being taken over by nationals – were leaving the country.

There had been two golf courses in Wewak prior to the present one. One, active in the 1960s, was a country club that, in addition to a 9-hole golf course, had a bowling green. It was not a very good course, built as it was in a marshy area. Consequently, most people played at the other course located at the Moem Army Base. This was "a really nice one with a fine clubhouse on the beach." But after Independence there was a falling out with the Commanding Officer, who was "not interested in golf and didn't much like either civilians or white people." Perhaps because of these strained relations, he decided that if outsiders were to be allowed on the base to play, then the club's board of directors had to be exclusively army personnel. Although the club had been "run well" for a long time, very soon after this change the "money was knocked off" and then there was a nasty incident in which "someone got very drunk and chucked half the trophies [displayed behind the bar] into the sea."

At this point, Prime Minister Michael Somare – who happened to be an avid golfer (and from the East Sepik) – called a meeting to discuss what to do about golf in Wewak. He and seven other town leaders – three Papua New Guineans, three Chinese and two Europeans – decided to develop a new golf course. They included business owners, a bank manager and an engineer for the Public Works Department. (The engineer eventually designed and supervised the construction of the course and clubhouse.) The course was built on land (somehow) acquired from the army: it was land reserved for military training, but never in fact used for that purpose. Local people, our expat source continued, though they had sold the land to the government long before, still pursued claims to it. Indeed, there had recently been a disruption at the course, when the claimants smashed some windshields and threatened other trouble. Somare was present at the time and his bodyguard fired his gun in the direction of these claimants. While this was going on, the golfers hid under the tables. On the following day, locals charged out of the church located across from the course, grabbed golf clubs and began flailing around with them. Regardless of these disputes and regardless of the circumstances by which the army and then the club had acquired the land, full title was finally transferred to the club in 1993. This was some five years after completion of the course and incorporation of the club.

To finance the project, Somare "leaned on big corporations" like Burns Philp and British Petroleum. He told them that they had not sponsored anything major in Wewak and it was time they did. Many local companies also gave money and in addition "bought a hole for K1,000." To build the course "a lot of government machinery was used as usual in Papua New Guinea" on such projects – especially projects thought of as "having public benefit." About 100 hectares of land were drained and cleared. According to our expat informant, the engineer for Works produced a "lousy design: all the holes run east to west so when the course is used most – after work and early in the morning on weekends – people have the sun in their eyes."

5. Some thought the Wewak clubhouse was not very secure – having been "built thirty years too late."

And while the clubhouse (a very large, open-sided room, raised fifteen feet from the ground on massive wooden posts) was a beautiful structure, it was not very secure – having been "built thirty years too late." He was referring to recent problems created by impoverished locals and disgruntled youths living in nearby squatter settlements.

Even though government equipment and workers were used for the project, by the time the course and clubhouse were finished, members had a debt of K60,000. They tried to pay it off with social nights and raffles (comparable to the Rotary dinner-auction), but these barely covered the interest. Then our informant decided to organize gambling nights, primarily on the outcome of Australian sporting events such as horse races and rugby finals. These proved successful and the club's hefty percentage of the wagers virtually paid off the debt. (Such events have continued, we shall see, as much for their social as for their financial benefits.)

The course has remained popular. It was used throughout the week: during the relative cool of the early mornings and late afternoons on weekdays and all day on the weekends. For instance, we would often see our neighbors leave their home, which was

6. We would often see our neighbors leave their home, which was secured by guard dogs and an electric-gated fence, to drive to the club in their air-conditioned Toyota 4Runner for a weekend game.

secured by guard dogs and an electric-gated fence, to drive to the club in their air-conditioned Toyota 4Runner for a weekend game. A couple working for Wewak's Westpac bank, he (a fellow Rotarian) as manager, she as officer in charge of corporate accounts, they were among the most affluent of Wewak's middle class. Both Tolai from East New Britain, the husband was a university-trained economist (who was initially educated as a priest); his wife had been trained as a schoolteacher. They played golf not only because they enjoyed it, but, for him it was a way of meeting people concerned with business. He liked being able to go to the club and just play with anyone ready to tee off – and, then, when walking down the fairway, he and his golfing companions could easily "talk about anything you want to, including business."

The most avid woman golfer we encountered in Wewak, also a banker and also originally trained as a teacher, was assistant manager of Wewak's branch of the Papua New Guinea Banking Corporation. (She was soon to be transferred to Goroka as manager.) Her father, from a Sepik River village, had been a policeman stationed throughout the country. (He had been a good friend of Michael Somare's father, as well a policeman. Indeed, she and Michael Somare had partially grown up together and he had given her away at her wedding.) She had been brought up largely in Port Moresby. When her Milne Bay husband was transferred to Wewak in the mid-1980s as an assistant secretary in the provincial government, she moved back to her home province and took a job at the bank. Since returning to the East Sepik, she had only been to her Sepik River village of origin twice, once shortly after she arrived and once when her father died. She and her family – her four sons, her husband and her mother (who lived near them in a house they had provided) – were all interested in sports. The two youngest boys played soccer, for example, at the International School. Though expensive, they went there because in her words, "what kind of education would they get in a classroom of sixty-five students which is what [the public education at] St. Mary's is up to." In addition, the International School sent them home with interesting books. These they were to read with their parents' assistance and supervision. Not only did this family read together, but – when not at the golf club – they would often picnic and swim together at the beach. Golf was, however, her special pleasure: she liked "worrying about a little ball and nothing else after a hard day at the office." Moreover, as had been the case in Wewak, she expected that at her new job in Goroka, golf would help her "meet lots of people."

Two Wewak golfers (among the relatively few with whom we actually played) were particularly forthcoming about their perspectives on life, and about how golf related to them. These were a husband and wife who were co-owners of several Wewak enterprises, including a restaurant, a guest house, a trade store, and a cacao and coconut plantation. Interested as we were in Wewak's Papua New Guinea elite, we had sought them out at their store especially in order to meet the wife (whom we mentioned in chapter 1): she was the daughter of a famous leader – a war hero, and a long-time supporter of educational and economic "development." Although (as a fervent Pentecostal) she attributed her own achievements in business ultimately to God, who had "maneuvered" her life so as to make success possible, she also believed that family influences were very important. She explained that her father, hating laziness, dependence on handouts and lack of initiative, believed a person had to earn what she or he got through sweat and through making choices. Correspondingly, she said, he objected to bride price arrangements and payments, although he would tell people that the bride prices of his many daughters could have made him rich. He viewed his children as special gifts from God and wanted them to marry anyone they chose – and to do so freely. She herself had chosen her present husband. This was after her first marriage had failed, when she decided to leave medical school for a career as an airline hostess.

Her husband, for his part, was a trained agriculturalist from Madang. He had worked for the Department of Lands and on privately owned plantations, and was responsible for revivifying her father's plantation. More recently, he had completed the select training program for aspiring retailers, known as *Stret Pasin Stoakipa* (Straight Practicing Storekeepers), and was awaiting final certification that he (and she) had at last repaid the debts he had incurred for the store he had been "loaned" through the program. As soon as this "freedom" was won, he would pursue his true vocation, developing an indigenous gospel music. He thought it a pity that Papua New Guinea musicians sang, for example, Jimmy Swaggart songs. After all, he said, "Jimmy Swaggart's feelings are not mine." His own music expressed his feelings as "its basic foundation." He thought that because "today in Wewak is different from today in Australia or today in America, or even a long time ago for a whiteman, Papua New Guineans should not be using the songs written by those of other times and places."

After our first meeting at the store, we spoke to this couple many times – and often about golf. He played golf for many reasons: he really enjoyed "belting the ball"; golf took his mind away from everything else; and in playing golf he competed against himself and the course. He was not pleased that most of the expats playing the game had lower handicaps than the nationals. He had always liked to move into areas where "no nationals had been before," and he "publicized" the game, telling his friends that it was played on "our land" and, moreover, was a "good game." Further, to publicize the game he had taught many to play and they, in turn, had taught others. In teaching he showed players "the good and the bad" and then said, "Now you can choose; you are a unique person and you know what to do." In teaching, his son to drive a car he used a comparable technique. He showed him once, clearly, about the clutch, brake, and accelerator and then watched him "struggle and sweat." If his son did not do well he would say, "You should have been listening."

He was always forceful and thoroughly self-assured in his badinage with fellow club members, and he was always vigilant in his proprietorial concern about the physical condition of the grounds. He played several times a week, often by himself, both to enjoy the physical activity in this serene location and to improve his handicap. In particular, he wished to prepare himself for the "opens" in Wewak and in other Papua New Guinea towns. He regularly attended these opens and competed for prizes. When we played with him, we found him a highly serious player, though tolerant of us as we – rank amateurs – struggled. He felt, however, frequently stymied by his caddies' lack of alacrity and attention. They apparently lacked the traits he so obviously valued both off the course and on – Tiger Woods' traits – of discipline, hardwork, and preparation. Once, while curtly telling them to use their heads and put a move on it, we were startled to see him snap his fingers at them. This was a colonial gesture we had not witnessed for decades in Papua New Guinea – and never between Papua New Guineans.

On families, feelings, and national networks

Most of the Papua New Guinea members of the Wewak Resort and Country Club whom we interviewed – indeed, most of Wewak's more affluent middle class – had similar social profiles. To restate the characteristics we mentioned in chapter 1: they were generally the children of men who had worked for the government or for the mission; they had been brought up in towns – frequently away from their home provinces; they usually had tertiary educations; they often married people from similar backgrounds, but not usually from their own cultural groups; they occasionally visited their villages of origin if they had parents living there; they rarely returned "home" once their parents died, or once they brought their parents to live with them in town. And, like the middle-class members of Rotary and SWIT, the Papua New Guinean golfers stressed the complexity of their relationships with less-affluent and less-educated relatives. All recognized that kin demands for economic assistance could mean financial ruin unless properly controlled. Most had established stringent rules to regulate these demands, lest they be "pulled down." Many sought to educate their kin, those still living in villages or squatter settlements, about the nature of their urban life: they stressed to them that running a business took discipline, hard work and preparation and that they had to meet special expenses.

Wewak's golfers, Rotarians, and affluent SWIT members shared another important characteristic. Along with mediating (though rarely entirely repudiating) connections with impecunious kin, these affluent members of the middle class also sought ties with (often distant) relatives and others comparable to themselves. These were ties which augmented rather than diminished their capacity to display and to consume. They sought to create and nurture connections with like achievers, not only locally but nationally (sometimes internationally) – connections that allowed them to confirm and to perpetuate their status as the middle-class elite. Certainly, many of our middle-class friends were assiduous in maintaining connections with *successful* friends and acquaintances. These might be from their own cultural group or locale. Or they might be those they knew while attending high school and university. Or they might have been associated with them on previous jobs. Or, they might be those they came to know in contexts of affable and affluent sociability at venues such as the golf club.

Maintaining a network of widely dispersed connections to other affluent nationals was often facilitated by placing classified or sometimes full-page commemorative ads in national newspapers. These were of themselves conspicuous acts of display and consumption. (Three out of four of these national newspapers were English-language. Consequently, the majority of Papua New Guineans could not even read them, much less afford to advertise in them.) Indeed, precisely as those of the urban middle class were becoming significantly less involved in the life-crisis ceremonies of their village or squatter settlement kin, they engaged in an emerging urban practice of placing newspaper notices focused on the births, deaths and birthdays of the affluent. For example, under an incredibly cute picture of Sean Wesley Walaur Varily, described as "Alias 'Tonton,'" happy first birthday wishes were presented by a large number of his dispersed and apparently well-placed relatives, including uncles and aunts at Papua New Guinea's two (and highly restrictive) universities (*Independent*, 1996: 26). Comparably, deaths – especially for those in, or connected to, government service – were marked by full- or half-page messages from a range of politicians and civil servants sending, for example, "heartfelt condolences to Mr. Tau Peruka, immediate family and relatives on the death of their father the late Peruka Mea" (*National*, 1996b: 30).

Such ads could be understood as helping construct a national community – both actual and "imagined" (Anderson, 1983) – of members of a middle-class elite who were kept informed about, and could participate in, the lives of those comparable to themselves, whether they happened, in fact, to know them or not (cf. Foster, 1995). It is important to note, moreover, that the national newspapers themselves sometimes solicited statements reflecting (and, presumably, effecting) a vision, not just of the appropriate sociality, but of the concomitant sensibility, of this national culture.

For instance, ideology about the affective ties within nuclear – nuclearizing – families was displayed and fostered by newspapers as they instructed readers in a calendricality of consumption and sentiment. Mother's Day, for one,[3] was nationally promoted by the press both as a time to express material appreciation (often through the gift of a domestic appliance) and as a time to express sentimental appreciation for a mother's affective centrality in a nuclear family's often inward-looking emotional economy.[4] Thus, under the caption "For Mum" and a picture of a Papua New Guinean mother there was printed the following poem, in excellent English. It had been submitted by Roger Brian for a newspaper-run competition and had won him a T-shirt. (The other two winners, with comparable though apparently slightly superior contributions, each received a Walkman.)

When nightmares have awakened me late into the night;
You're the one who's held my hand and made everything all right.
Yet, so often I neglect to tell you how I feel;
To thank you for all the love you gave with tender zeal.
But how can I tell you of the things I feel inside;
Of how having you for my Mum, makes my heart swell with pride?
So, though I seldom say these things I always know they are a part
Of the love I hold for you each day within my heart. (Brian, 1996: 30)

Conveyed here is the image of a close family in which children were given every advantage, both emotional and intellectual. The newspaper reader would likely imagine that Roger's parents felt it was important to pay the steep tuition for his International School education and to make sure his homework was done. Perhaps his mother had, following school instructions, read with him. Certainly his parents would recognize that their input had an important effect in conveying to him the importance of discipline, hard work and preparation.

To be sure, we knew many mothers of International School children who did not read with them. And to be sure, we knew many fathers who, as drunken, poker-machine playing, womanizers, were less than upstanding role models. Yet, affluent members of the Papua

New Guinea middle class were, nonetheless, at least loosely bound together by the idea – and, to some extent, the fact – that there existed a community of elite national families with a comparable social and sentimental organization.

Such a social and sentimental organization was, as the profiles of Wewak golfers have suggested, embraced by many members of the Wewak Resort and Country Club. It was, as well, at golf-centered events (including the Wewak Open, to be described in the final section of the chapter), that Wewak's branch of this elite community became both verified and instantiated (as it was at the Rotary dinner-auction). Indeed, it was into this community (whether the Wewak or another branch) that Tiger Woods, his family and his AMEX card would have been most warmly welcomed.

Thus, although we suspect Woods would not have been much impressed with the Wewak golf scene, he would have found it familiar: he would have encountered the relatively standardized features of an international sport and he would have been able to find in this postcolonial Papua New Guinea setting recognizable aspects of (Euro-American-derived) middle-class culture. He would have found "unique person[s]" (to quote our aforementioned golfing companion) interested in establishing groups of friendly but serious competitors who were intent on freely chosen (not kin-based), fluid (noncorporate) sociality. He would have found in this middle-class enclave of elite Papua New Guineans, relatively mobile, stand-alone nuclear families (like his own), concerned with socialization, acquisition and consumption. He would have found friends whose social relations outside of the family were premised on the loose sociability of good company or on the network connections that, to remain ongoing, must remain of mutual socioeconomic benefit.[5]

On the margin

Michael Kamban, waiting on the margin for Paul Wanjik, his (Papua New Guinean) parliamentary representative to come to the course, was interested in a differently configured sociality – one with different emphases – than any which would have so readily included Tiger Woods into the Wewak Resort and Country Club. He had brought his family to Wewak, early in our 1996 fieldwork, so that his youngest son could receive medical assistance and so that he could claim the outboard motor Wanjik had promised him some four years before. As it happened, he was able to move in with his sister in a

7. Michael Kamban was interested in a differently configured sociality than any which would have readily included Tiger Woods into the Wewak Resort and Country Club.

squatter settlement adjacent to the golf course (where his older son began to caddy occasionally). Though months had begun to pass, Michael vowed that he would not return to his Chambri Island home until his son was cured and the debt was settled. In the meantime, he hoped that his wife could earn enough money in Wewak selling food to golfers (and artifacts to tourists) in order to support them and perhaps to buy a few necessities such as clothes, batteries and kerosene, items that were hard (or expensive) to acquire on Chambri.

We had known Michael for years. Of the four research assistants who had aided Deborah during her initial (1974–75) study, he was the only one who had remained primarily in the Chambri village of his birth. Laconic, wry and smart, he had provided us in both conversation and in letters and essays with insight into the possibilities and problems of maintaining a village-based identity. Such an identity, he now told us as he visited us in our Wewak house, had become impossible to sustain without cash. Indeed, he wanted money from us, not only to support him in Wewak, but to help him start a small business at home, a business catching, smoking and transporting fish. He hoped either to sell or to trade these fish. One possibility was to trade fish for lumber, which he could either use or sell at Chambri.

Michael expected our help. After all, we had a long history of mutual entailment – of reciprocity – going back over twenty years. Originally Deborah had exchanged money for his research assistance in recording Chambri expenditures at the Catholic mission-owned trade store on Chambri Island. These initial transactions had ramified over the years and involved gifts of watches, photographs, a pressure lamp, a tent, clothing and money from us and companionship, protection, information, letters, essays, artifacts and food from him and his family.

Thus, out of ongoing entailment, we promptly took his son to a private clinic and purchased rather expensive medicine and vitamins for him. This much having been done, it then became virtually impossible not to contribute money and food to him and his family. Moreover, as Michael requested, we gave him a fishing net for his proposed business. However, since the outboard motor he still wanted was (at almost K2,000) beyond our research budget (especially since such a purchase would have fueled comparable requests from numerous Chambri), we agreed to help him get the one he claimed to be owed from Paul Wanjik. Wanjik had promised the motor in return for Michael's extensive help during his last campaign. Another election was imminent, and Michael knew that he did not have much time to compel payment: if Wanjik won, he would have a whole new set of obligations to pay; if he lost, he would have neither money nor inclination to fulfill any of his debts, old or new. Our job was to type a letter Michael had written (in Neo-Melanesian) to compel Wanjik to reciprocate before it was too late.

This letter recounted the amount of money (K1,082) for fuel and parts, as well as the amount of time (several weeks) Michael spent transporting Wanjik and his election team from village to village throughout the Chambri Lake area. It also listed those who had heard Wanjik promise to give Michael a new Yamaha 25-horsepower outboard motor and enumerated the times Michael had tried to get him to fulfill his promise. Michael mailed and faxed copies of this letter to Wanjik at both his Port Moresby and Wewak offices. When he received no reply, he began, copies in hand, to haunt the peripheries of the hotels, clubs and the golf course where Wanjik would likely visit when in town.

Michael also began to document for us the full extent to which he claimed Wanjik had reneged on obligations to his constituents. He did this, we think, both to repay us for the money we continued to give him and his family for sustenance in Wewak, and to justify his sense of grievance. In all, he wrote almost 100 pages. He described in close detail and sequence, Wanjik's campaign visits throughout the region: how villagers from *each* (and every) specific community had welcomed him with dances, banquets, speeches and gifts of artifacts; what villagers had told Wanjik they required of their representative, such as aid posts, schools and economic "help"; what Wanjik promised he would deliver (seemingly whatever it took to get the vote); and how nothing had been forthcoming after the election. Below we provide (in minimally edited translation from the Neo-Melanesian) a single example of what was, in fact, an epic deconstruction of Wanjik's electoral campaign and triumph.

Wombun community

In 1992, there were national elections in Papua New Guinea. In every province there were people who ran against one another within their constituencies. Within the Wosera-Gawi constituency, there were many candidates. One was Paul Wanjik from Wosera, from the village of Wambisa. He brought his campaign to the Chambri Lakes.

When he arrived at [the Chambri village of] Wombun, the people there were ready to greet him. They had rehearsed traditional dances, which they planned to perform at the Walindimi men's house. They had also decorated a large chair in ancestral fashion. In the past, only a big man would sit on such a chair to proclaim about matters of concern to the people, such as warfare. In addition, members of the Wombun community prepared a string bag, to place around Paul Wanjik's shoulder, in which they had put betel nut and pepper, a bamboo lime holder and tobacco. Also in the bag were two pig tusks and other ancestral decorations. All of these gifts were prepared to mark the community of Wombun within Paul's memory if he won the election.

When he arrived, the community welcomed him: the cultural group performed dances for him after which he was led inside the men's house and seated in the ceremonial chair. Members of the community then expressed their concerns. First, they wanted Paul to promise that he would help them get government money to complete the Walindimi men's house. This he said he would do. Second, they wanted fish nets for the women of Wombun, so that they might use them to earn a little money to help their families. Paul promised that he had already ordered nets from Japan. Third, they wanted an outboard motor for the community because many people need help getting their fish to markets ... Transportation is a big problem for the people of the Chambri Lakes. Paul promised the motor; in fact, he had already ordered this too. Then, Cleopas Kolly asked about his guest house. He wanted some money so that his clan project could proceed. He mentioned that when Paul's campaign supporters traveled in the area, they had slept in this guest house without charge. And Mr. Cleopas reminded Paul that the house needed repairs and this took money. Paul assured him that, when he was elected, money would be forthcoming. Others spoke about the need of Chambri children for health services ... And Paul promised these as well. In particular, he promised that he would build a small hospital in the Chambri Lakes.

So these were the concerns of the people of Wombun which they conveyed to Paul Wanjik and his secretary, Tony Dimi of Burui Village in the Pagwi subdistrict. And Tony recorded these concerns with his own hand. And Paul heard them as he sat in the ceremonial chair. And all the people of Chambri saw the welcome that the Wombun Community provided for Mr. Paul Wanjik. They saw him go inside the men's house and what happened afterwards. When all the talk was finished, Mr. Yambai of Japandai Village, who was on the Pangu Party [Wanjik's party] electoral committee, asked for a cultural performance group to accompany Paul as he paid his nomination fee at Maprik. This group was composed of members from all three Chambri villages. They went at their own expense – by boat to Pagwi and then by truck to Maprik . . .

After the fee was paid, Paul won the election and went to Parliament. He did this with the power and strength and talk of the Wombun Community of Chambri Lakes. And did he think once about the hard work of the people of Wombun? Did he do a single thing or provide any help – a single project – to repay the people? After he got his position, did he think once of the *kanaka* [backward villagers] of Wombun in the Chambri Lakes?

No, there hasn't been a single bit of help during the five years he has been in national government. Not one act of help – I swear it, in the name of Almighty God in heaven. We voted for him – why? So he could become rich and sleep with lots of women in Port Moresby? Or play around in the town with his cronies? So, the people of Wombun feel deeply hurt because they have simply been discarded as rubbish by Paul Wanjik.

Michael was outraged because Wanjik had engaged with and then repudiated both Michael himself and the sociality in which Michael derived meaning and orientation. What was explicitly created by Wanjik's visit to the villages of the Wosera-Gawi electorate – at least according to Michael's deconstruction of these visits – was an imagined community of socially and spatially located peoples with long and twisted histories of reciprocity (like those histories still compelling the basket weavers described in chapter 2). This reciprocity had, to be sure, not only the positive aspects of barter markets, intermarriage and trading partnerships; it had, as well, negative aspects of warfare, sorcery and sometimes bitter competition for regional prestige. But in either regard, it was a history of groups taking each other seriously in ways they knew would ramify and shape both present and future. In such a world, a massive defaulter on obligation like Wanjik *should* be in serious social disrepute, if not in physical danger. Yet, to the indignation of Michael and, presumably, many other Wosera-Gawi villagers, Wanjik did not become a rubbishy defaulter; he had instead managed to discard them as rubbish, as all nonentities relative to his affluent, urban friends.

Michael would not accept himself as rubbish and so, on arrival in Wewak, began a vigil outside the venues of middle-class sociality, trying to catch Wanjik on his infrequent and generally unannounced visits to his home province. Once Michael came upon him drinking at a hotel, but Wanjik escaped into a guest room before Michael could state his grievances and hand him the letter providing written documentation of his case. On another occasion, waiting by the golf course early in the morning, Michael saw, not Wanjik, but Michael Somare, Wanjik's political superior,[6] preparing for a game. Approaching, he explained about Wanjik's debt to him. Somare (apparently) listened attentively and accepted the letter enumerating Michael's grievances. He then told Michael that because Wanjik had made a "commitment," he must pay his debt. Michael was jubilant. He told us that, because Wanjik was no match for Somare, he would settle up immediately.

But as time continued to pass without any results, various people began strongly urging Michael to take his family back to Chambri. We were getting tired of supporting him in Wewak in what we felt was an entirely fruitless quest; and other Chambri were getting annoyed both with us and with him since they thought more of our support should be going to them. We eventually advised him to cut his losses and go home, explaining that Wanjik would likely never give him the outboard motor. Indeed, we asked, why should he? Wanjik in his efforts to win votes had obviously promised vastly more than he could deliver and this meant he would necessarily be in default to almost everyone. Why, out of this sea of unfulfilled obligation, would he single out Michael for repayment?[7] Michael was, after all, only one vote.

In his turn, Michael had been getting angry with us (and, to a lesser extent, with other Chambri) for not supporting him enough both materially and in his quest. Moreover, he found infuriating our analysis that, as only one vote, he had virtually no capacity to elicit payment from Wanjik. For us to describe his efficacy as that of only one vote showed our lack of commitment to the social world of commensurate differences, a social world that gave him potential significance as a contender. We were suggesting that his efforts to achieve a vindication of either glory or revenge were inherently unlikely to succeed: that he was unlikely to be one who, virtually alone in Wosera-Gawi, could compel Wanjik to pay up; that he was also unlikely to be one who, if Wanjik did not pay up, could effectively reveal him to all as rubbish. Thus, we were suggesting that Wanjik would remain, at least for the duration of his term in office, relatively powerful; that Michael would remain, probably for the duration of his life, outboard-motorless and, in increasingly important contexts, inadequate. We were, in effect, telling Michael that, as a village *kanaka*, he could never, in a Papua New Guinea of growing incommensurate differences, pull off the coup he so keenly sought.

The Wewak Open

During the last weekend of May 1996, over 200 members and guests of the golf club streamed past Michael and some of his squatter-settlement acquaintances watching from the margin of the course parking lot. It was the local golfing occasion of the year, the two-day Wewak Open. The events of exclusion for Michael and his companions were events of inclusion for members and guests: the ethos of comfortable familiarity these insiders experienced, the easy, good humored bantering, might have characterized any family oriented, community-focused festivity in small-town America or Australia.

Many, though fewer than half of the members and guests attending, had actually come to play golf. (Those who did come to play golf had paid K60 to compete in the tournament.) As it was both customary and polite for Papua New Guinea's golfers to try to attend each other's opens, one female and twenty-eight male players from other golf clubs joined the six female and twenty-eight male players from Wewak's club. The visitors were mostly, to be sure, from the relatively nearby Mount Hagen club. (Correspondingly, fifteen Wewak golfers had the previous month played at Mount Hagen's open at the cost, we estimate, of about K300 each.) But even for those playing, and all the more so for those just watching or organizing, much of the weekend of the open was spent in convivial socializing.

Filling the clubhouse ornamented for the occasion with advertising banners donated by such corporate sponsors as South Pacific Beer, British Petroleum and Toyota, the members and guests were clearly enjoying themselves: they sat in small groups or strolled around, talking, drinking beer, eating sandwiches and fried chicken (prepared by several golfing wives); they looked approvingly at the table full of trophies and prizes donated by local merchants (luggage, golf equipment, watches, small appliances). They also participated in numerous club fund-raisers. Most would spend K5 or K10 on raffle tickets, which might win them a bottle of rum or whiskey. Some, either as individuals or as members of quickly assembled "syndicates," would bid hundreds of kina for a chance to win club-constructed pools based on golfing outcomes.

They watched, sometimes applauding, the shots of nearby golfers. They commented about the state of play: how someone (generally the speaker) had done relative to his hopes and expectations and, more broadly, who was on or off his (sometimes her) game. And they

8. Prizes and awards were given in convivial ambiance at the closing proceedings of the Wewak Open.

mentioned frequently the soggy condition of the course. Several times we heard amused references to the beginning of the tournament itself when, the rain having just stopped, Somare and two of the club's officers set out: the club's captain had quipped to Somare that he should feel right at home since the course must remind him of his (swampy) Murik Lakes' village. Hearing this story recounted, others joked in their turn that next year's players should bring gum boots rather than golf shoes to Wewak.

The closing proceedings in which the prizes and awards were given were comparable in convivial ambience. First, club officers warmly thanked the sponsors, dignitaries and other supporters for their help. These included the expat director of British Petroleum in Papua New Guinea (thanked for providing subsidized fuel for the golf-course tractor as well as other assistance), visiting Papua New Guinea politicians (thanked for their illustrious presence) and certain local members (thanked for trucking in sand to fill especially boggy places near the clubhouse and for allowing their "better halfs" to prepare and serve the food). Then, club officers spoke briefly about the excellent fiscal health of the Wewak club, as well as the desirability of promoting golf as an "important game," a game that "provided a way for lots of people to meet, including [those] from different races." And then came the lengthy presentations of many different minor and major prizes: a small trophy and four golf balls went to the female golfer who drove the ball nearest to the pin on the 8th hole on the first day; a large trophy and minor appliance went to the female golfer who had the best handicapped score on the first and second days; an elaborate traveling cup went to the male golfer who had the best (nonhandicapped) overall score. Announcements of the more important awards were greeted with cheers or with groans, depending on whether the recipient was from the home club or elsewhere

Indeed, with the visitors, especially those from Mount Hagen, claiming triumph over their Wewak hosts, the evening ended with a chorus of exaggerated claims and excuses and jovial challenges of "just wait until next year." Nor was the evening of convivial socializing marred by any unpleasant discoveries in the parking lot. Perhaps because special security had been employed for the occasion, no windshields had been smashed or other damage done during the evening.

Conclusion

In the Papua New Guinea of 1996 there were many "Michaels" of different ages and commitments to rural or urban lives. They lurked on the margins of middle-class contexts of affluent sociality such as the Wewak Resort and Country Club, waiting for their chance. Tiger Woods and American Express might have argued that giving poor Papua New Guineans – youth especially – the opportunity to learn golf could provide one such chance: through golf, they could acquire not just the discipline, hard work and preparation requisite for success, but also the entry into the affluent sociability that marked success. Such success would, of course, have to be largely confirmed and maintained by the degree to which they and their nuclear families achieved the capacity to consume (even to perilous levels of indebtedness) – including the capacity to consume through golf itself.

Woods and American Express would, in fact, have been right in some things and wrong in others concerning Wewak. They would have been right that Wewak and Papua New Guinea have increasingly been caught up in worldwide processes of class formation and consumption. And, they would have been right that these processes and the incommensurate differences they produced could be ideologically justified in globally familiar terms. Those who were successful and those who were not were increasingly thought of, especially by the successful, as different sorts of people having different sorts of characteristics: the affluent had personal qualities such as discipline, hard work and preparation; the poor had personal qualities such as lack of focus, laziness, and inadequate planning. Hence, as we saw in chapter 2, there was increasing assurance in Papua New Guinea (certainly by the successful) that, because success and failure stemmed from personal traits and therefore were equitably distributed, both success and the company of the successful could be enjoyed without misgivings.

Woods and American Express would also have been right in believing that it was in contexts such as Wewak's golf club that such values and corresponding socialities became realized – became both instantiated and recognized. And, as we have suggested, it was in such affluent contexts that an imagined community of the Papua New Guinea successful acquired enhanced tangibility – a community of those sharing lifestyle patterns evoked in part through the national media in, for example, birthday ads and Mother's Day tributes. It was, in other words, through such contexts that this imagined community took actual sociocultural form, through the easy, unentailed, mutually confirmative sociality of unrelated, like-minded, nuclear family focused, comparably successful men and women engaged in golf, banter, fund-raising and drinking.

However, although Woods and American Express might have been right in banking on the direction in which they thought much of the world was moving, they would have been wrong in their implied assumption that everyone wanted the world to go this way except the failures – those lacking discipline, hard work and preparation. Michael, after all, had a different sociality in mind and, moreover, lacked none of these virtues. What he eschewed was the kind of individuality which measured worth by the capacity to consume primarily within nuclear (nuclearizing) families and by the capacity to limit socializing primarily to carefully selected and well-positioned others. His desire for an outboard motor stemmed as much from his insistence to be taken seriously in a relationship as from his wish to start a fish business. And, if he did manage to start this business, he would have little expectation of educating his kin to respect the autonomy necessary for him to run it "successfully." Since his was an imagined community of socially and spatially located peoples with long and twisted histories of reciprocity, his success would be measured largely by his capacity to fulfill, not to repudiate, kin and other claims.

The alternative sociality that Michael embraced meant, virtually by definition in contemporary Papua New Guinea, that he would never gain access to serious resources – since those with serious resources did not need anything from Michael (except perhaps his one vote – and a chance to exploit him as a boat driver). Moreover, even if Michael's son did somehow "make it" (unlikely, given the workings of class, even if he received some local golfing scholarship), all except his closest kin would be cut out of the benefits, lest he be "pulled down." Such a turning of events might well have been inexorable in Papua New Guinea. But it would take some time for the great majority of Papua New Guineans to accept this turning of events as any simple product of discipline, hard work and preparation. A future of broken windshields would very likely attest to that.

From one perspective, the triumph of American Express over its multinational rivals in claiming Tiger Woods' multicultural face as its own could, indeed, be regarded as one sort of "coup." However, it might also be regarded as a coup of another sort – a coup that indexed a more violent worldwide displacement from public attention of less welcome faces – Michael's included.[8]

In the next chapter, we see another such displaced face – that belonging to our old friend and colleague, Godfried Kolly (see Gewertz and Errington, 1991a and 1996). Like Michael, Godfried had come to experience the elusive nature of the desirable in a Papua New Guinea where imported socialities – in Godfried's case, his consumption-mediated relationships with middle-class soccer referees – were the only appropriate contexts for the establishment of efficacious identities. Godfried's story not only provides additional information concerning those grass-roots individuals unable to achieve such identities. It also, in its focus on the social life of desirable things, helps us understand more about why he (and others) should so profoundly wish such identities.

4
The hidden injuries of class

Desiring the unattainable

We have been demonstrating the effects of a system of incommensurate differences on the lives of Papua New Guineans – both on members of the middle class and on those of the grass roots, increasingly defined (by SWIT-like rhetorics) as the blameworthy poor. In the last chapter, we conveyed the wrenching consequences of exclusion on one of our Chambri friends, as he patrolled the margins of middle-class sociality seeking, unsuccessfully, his due. In this chapter we continue to portray – to embody – the hidden (and not so hidden) injuries of class exclusion. The story we tell of Godfried Kolly's attempt to achieve middle-class acceptance – to achieve what was, in effect, a glory day of entrepreneurial success so as to win friends – may be even more telling of contemporary social processes in Papua New Guinea than Michael's. Perhaps because Godfried was a town dweller, his efforts were less directed toward defying and challenging class distinctions than toward accommodating to their existence. Godfried's story teaches us, in other words, what happens to the poor when class has become a *fait accompli.*

To understand the social and economic dimensions of Godfried's entrepreneurial efforts in capitalist Wewak, we begin this chapter with a reference to another, earlier and more durable global emissary than the multicultural, postcolonial Tiger Woods – to James Leahy, one of the initial white explorers to engage with Papua New Guinea Highlanders. Both Leahy and Woods provide informative contrasts to Godfried, ones which, we think, clarify well the (often) invidious nature of the transformations within a global economy of a system of commensurate to one of incommensurate differences.

First contact

In the film, *First Contact,* James Leahy justified his and his brothers' 1930s expedition and its effects – both immediate and long-lasting – by unabashed reference to economic self-interest (Connolly and Anderson, 1984). He said that he had not come to Papua New Guinea for his health and, indeed, did not much like either the climate or the people. Yet, he cheerfully asserted, he had not done too badly for himself. Not only Europeans but Papua New Guineans, he thought, had an interest in commerce. Indeed, the members of the Leahy expedition, threading their way through mountain valleys in search of gold, had carried shells and trade goods to acquire provisions and labor from those they encountered. Reminiscing about a seemingly inexorable course of capitalist efficacy – one explaining as well as justifying the control (sometimes killing) of natives and the appropriation of land for mining operations and airfields – James explained that Papua New Guineans were "wild for the trade."

Given the importance for Melanesians of objects in establishing personal/social efficacy, it was not surprising that these Highlanders showed substantial interest in those items the Leahys imported. Several scenes from *First Contact* depicted local fascination with ordinary Western commodities – indeed commodities so ordinary as to have been simply thrown away by members of the expedition. For example, one picture was of a Papua New Guinea man wearing the front of a discarded cereal box as a headdress. In another scene, an elderly man described how, as a youth, he had surreptitiously removed a tin-can lid from the Leahy encampment, only to have his prize claimed first by his uncle and then by his father, so keen were their desires for it.[1]

In their evocation of avid local desire for imported goods, such depictions could be understood as parables of the nature of entrepreneurial opportunity. They were, in effect, renditions of charter myths for global traders, for those with the fortitude and vision to travel the world to find and seize the maximally advantageous moment. They provided axiomatic examples of the desirably anomalous: those first on the scene with the right product could make a killing, could strike it rich. Indeed, it was in these first (or early) contacts that the intrepid might sometimes find the quintessential apotheosis of the global trader: find one's trash becoming another's treasure.

To understand why Godfried Kolly became "wild for the trade" in contemporary Papua New Guinea – about why he had both in person and through emissaries scoured the world to find and import objects which would strongly excite his desires and, by extrapolation, those of his compatriots – we must explore the "legacy" left by these global traders. This, as we shall see, was a legacy which included the subsequent local adoption – and adaptation – of the charter myths of first-contact entrepreneurial opportunity.[2]

In seeking to interpret Godfried's interests and objectives, we should recognize that being "wild for the trade" must be understood in terms of local comprehensions that were historically contingent. Certainly first-contacted Highlanders did not regard everything the Leahys offered as uniformly desirable. Strathern has in fact argued that the trade items which *most* engaged these Highlanders were not the novel but the known and already valued. Specifically, they were pearl shells (Strathern, 1992). Moreover, standards of local evaluation were, of course, subject to change over time. In this regard, and of direct relevance to understanding global social processes such as modernization and capitalism, it must be realized that local meanings of objects often became constrained or otherwise affected by larger contexts of meaning and use. And these contexts were at best under only partial local control. For instance, given the rapidly increasing weight of a colonial presence, when tin-can lids came to be locally understood as (literally) Australian garbage, they no longer were valued items of exchange.[3]

As this book has made clear, moreover, contemporary Papua New Guineans like Godfried no longer stood on the same ground, whether on the shores or in the Highland valleys, as did their predecessors encountering the initial global emissaries of the capitalist juggernaut (cf. Ortner, 1984). This did not in itself mean, however, that they were any less interested in the possibilities of global trade. But it did mean that some of the dynamics of that trade had changed. This was true not only because of shifts in what was locally regarded as the desirable. It was also – and relatedly – true because of an important reshuffling of those who had access to what kinds of desirable items. As we have seen, a colonial and postcolonial history of commodity (and other) transactions had also been a history of indigenous class happenings. (Some attended the Rotary dinner-auction; others did not. Some traveled to Jayapura; others could not.) As a consequence, the ground on which many Papua New Guineans found themselves had become increasingly uneven, shifting and uncertain. The "trade" that Godfried was "wild for" – and he was indeed blown away by the local possibilities of acquiring certain globally traversing objects – must therefore be understood as central to his strategy of achieving a place of assurance.

The transactions Godfried desired to make within world capitalism would be very much done for his "health" – to further his well-being with peoples (and in a climate) he generally enjoyed. However, because he lived in a capitalist history that was favoring some Papua New Guineans much more than others, his perfect entrepreneurial moment – evidently unlike James Leahy's – turned out to be an all-too-fleeting triumph and, hence, ultimately a tragedy. To fully interpret Godfried's effort to achieve his vision of a fully satisfying, contemporary reconfiguration of the global trader's entrepreneurial dream, a reconfiguration in which not just his "trade" but he himself became the embodiment of desire, we must first survey his own position on Papua New Guinea's late twentieth-century socioeconomic terrain.

Objects of desire

By the time of our 1996 field trip, 45-year-old Godfried had been living for some fifteen years relatively permanently at Chambri Camp. Nearly 30 percent of all Chambri had come to reside at this squatter settlement in Wewak, the capital of the East Sepik Province. Godfried had left his home village of Indingai, and with it his wife and three sons, in pursuit of a rather dangerous liaison: one which alienated him from his affines (to whom he had never completed bride price payments) and from (some of) his patrikin (as the liaison was with a rather closely related woman, a member of his own agnatic marriage moiety). Unwelcome in their home village, the two moved to the squatter settlement. After a few years and the birth of two daughters, they separated. Godfried moved in with – and came to be regarded as married to – yet another settlement-dwelling Chambri woman, with whom he had an additional three children.

Although trained in his youth to become an agricultural extension officer, Godfried never really held a full-time job. He had no regular income in Chambri Camp, and his life there was hard. Indeed, he and his children – all raggedly dressed and poorly fed – survived largely through gifts of food from home, remittances of money from kin (and us), earnings from his wife's sale of her handicrafts and meager profits from his desultory enterprises such as selling beer in the camp. His house was among the most ramshackle in the settlement, as he never troubled to patch it adequately. His relationship with his wife had deteriorated seriously: they fought constantly and she wanted him to leave so that she could marry a better provider. In order to escape her continual (and, we must grant, not entirely unfounded) tirades, he would travel to town every morning in his best clothes with the "shoe-sock" men – those of the middle class on their way to work (who wore shoes and socks to their jobs). People, he told us with a certain wryness, would often mistake him at such times for an employed civil servant.

Yet, his monetary and marital misfortunes notwithstanding, Godfried remained a proud man of many dimensions. He had spent nearly half of his life, off and on, as an anthropological research assistant, initially collecting demographic and economic data. During our fourth visit to the East Sepik in 1987, he began to call himself a "traditional anthropologist." Deciding that he was sufficiently versed in the profession to pursue independent studies, he immediately embarked on writing what he considered to be both an ethnography and the Chambri Bible. (His writings became the focus of a chapter about the politics of literacy and self-representation in *Twisted Histories, Altered Contexts* [Gewertz and Errington, 1991a].)

Subsequently, and just prior to our 1994 research, he registered as a "mastercrafts person" with the Department of Tourism and Culture. In his application, he described himself as an expert in dancing, carving and painting; also, he stated that, partly because of his research experience with us, he was proficient in collecting and transcribing traditional stories. By this time, and while he was still continuing in his role as "traditional anthropologist," he had become concerned with the preservation and presentation of Chambri "culture" (Gewertz and Errington, 1996). This concern had been fostered by his gratifying experiences a few years earlier, when he had toured Europe with other Chambri, performing traditional music and dances. By the time of our 1994 arrival, he had embarked on a plan whereby he, together with other members of the Chambri-based Yambai Culture Group, of which he was president, would travel throughout the Middle Sepik performing traditional music and dances in order to teach young people to learn and appreciate their key traditions. To implement this plan, he energetically (but unsuccessfully) sought sponsorship and financial support from various government and commercial organizations so that he might purchase a 15-horsepower outboard motor, two drums of gasoline, two amplifiers, one generator, three microphones and a sound mixer.

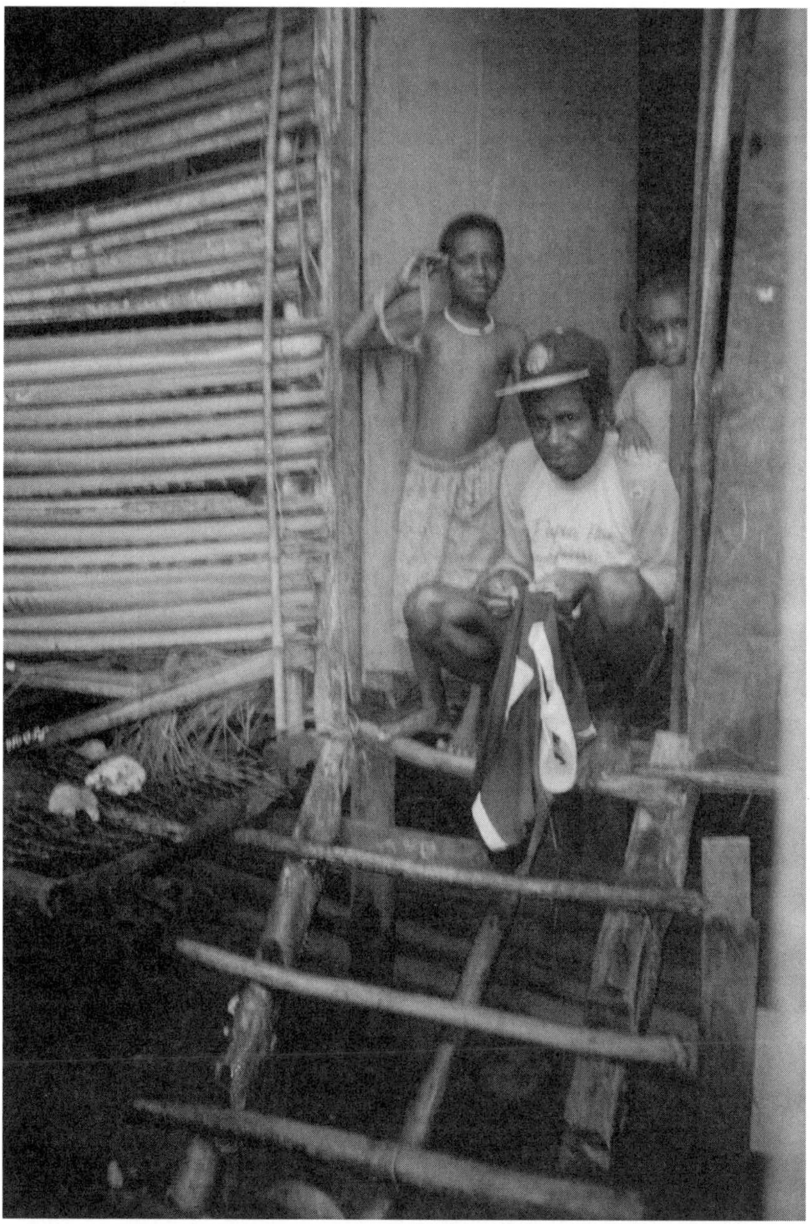

9. When Godfried Kolly became a Level Three soccer referee in 1994, he promptly sewed his official badge on his uniform as two of his children looked on.

Finally, also during the period of our 1994 research, he was engaged in another project of immense importance to him: to continue with his work as a "level three" soccer referee and, perhaps, to gain certification which would enable him to preside over international matches. It was in connection with his role as soccer referee that he later sought our help in acquiring those objects he had greatly come to desire: official – internationally recognized – referees' whistles.

Shortly before our return to Papua New Guinea in 1996, Godfried wrote asking us to bring him the whistles he needed. He stressed that they must be the "official" whistles, not the inadequate ones we had previously sent in response to his earlier letters during the previous two years. In pursuit of his objectives, we consulted the Amherst College soccer coach. After referring to an official guide listing whistles and other soccer accoutrements, he gave us twenty-seven whistles – whistles of three different (though equally official) types. In addition, he presented us with six soccer referees' jerseys. Pleased in anticipation of Godfried's pleasure, we wrote him that we would shortly be arriving in Papua New Guinea with what he had requested.

We include below (in translation from the Neo-Melanesian and with his permission) the essay he wrote (in his capacity as "traditional anthropologist") shortly after our arrival, concerning what had become objects of preoccupying desire for him. It is, in the following only slightly abridged form, a minor (though certainly passionate) treatise on the subject of virtual commodity-lust: of being truly "wild for the trade."

Official Referee Whistle

by Godfried Kolly

On Monday 15 January 1996 I received from America many whistles. These whistles my sister brought with my brother-in-law, Freddy. My sister is Deborah Gewertz. When the two of them arrived with 27 whistles and 6 black jerseys, I was very happy. All of these jerseys and whistles came from a coach in the United States who works in a university in America. I had written a sponsor letter to my sister Deborah and Freddy asking for help with whistles and jerseys.

They [earlier] sent a whistle together with a watch to me in Papua New Guinea. When I received this whistle and watch I was very happy with one of them – the watch. I liked the watch but I didn't like the whistle. I wanted another kind of whistle, a Fox 40. Not the whistle they sent, which I didn't like. OK. I then replied to the letter from Deborah and Freddy and told them that the watch was fine but the whistle was the wrong kind. I wanted a Fox 40 whistle with 3 holes. The watch they sent I had for only three weeks before some men stole it near the Wewak beach. They stole this watch on 18 January 1995. So I wrote again to Deborah Gewertz and told her that I want another watch – the same as the one she had sent. She sent two watches and when I received the two watches, together with two whistles, I wasn't happy. Because the two watches were the wrong ones altogether – they weren't the same as the first one she had sent. So I continued with my work of sending sponsor letters and finally Deborah got the idea and went to ask the soccer coach at the university in America. And the coach knew the whistles brother Godfried Kolly wanted were Fox 40s. And said that he would help. He wrote to the world sport coach and asked him for Fox 40 whistles and referee jerseys and he got them from the world sport coach in England. . . .

The night I knew the two of them had arrived in Papua New Guinea, I couldn't sleep. I wondered if they had brought the right whistles and thought of nothing else. At dawn the next day, on Sunday the 7th of January 1996, I got up very early, washed and went to Wirui Roman Catholic Church because I am a Roman Catholic. Just after church, I caught a bus . . . and went to town . . . to look for Deborah and Freddy. [On the bus] I met a young lady named Cisilia. As I was speaking to her about why she was on the bus, I didn't think about the whistles any longer or about the jerseys. For the whole day I went around with this woman and I didn't think very much about sister Deborah or Freddy or about all the whistles. I didn't think about them for about two days. Just after two days, Monday and Tuesday, I began again to try to find sister Deborah with Freddy. . . .

As soon as I saw them my first question was about the whistles. Deborah answered me that everything of yours, everything you requested, is at our house. So I went up the hill to the place where the two of them were staying and I got a parcel with 27 whistles and 6 jerseys. When I got this parcel I wondered if the whistles would be all right. Quickly I opened the parcel. The first one I looked at was the big one named Fox 40. At this time, at 12 o'clock on the 11th day of January 1996, I was very happy and proud. On this very day, on the 11th day of January at 12 o'clock, I knew that I had become a true referee. All my worries were gone as this is a big part of my life history.

It started in 1989, the time I became a referee in Papua New Guinea. I began to write letters to businesses [such as PepsiCo and South Pacific Holdings (brewers of South Pacific Beer)] and parliamentarians such as

Sir Michael Somare and Bernard Narakobi. But I didn't get one of them to sponsor me. No one. And in 1990, on the 5th day of May, I left Papua New Guinea and went to Europe. While I was in Europe for one month and three weeks, I tried to find whistles and jerseys. But I couldn't find any in the seven countries I visited in Europe – London, Holland, England, France and in all of the parishes in these countries. I looked and I couldn't find even one Fox 40 whistle and the same was true about jerseys. And I came back to Hong Kong where it was the same. And on the 31st of June 1990, the day I returned to Papua New Guinea, I was very worried about the whistles and jerseys – a worry which lasted for five years until 1995. . . .

So I am very happy about Deborah and Freddy . . . and I want to send big greetings to the national coach at the University in America at Amherst College. In addition, all the referees of the Wewak Soccer Referees Association are very happy to see that the first sponsor letter was effective. All of them have bought whistles from Godfried Kolly to make him happy for having gotten this support in the form of the whistles. The Fox 40 [draws a picture] I sold for K5 [K1 = about $US.80] and the other metal ones I gave away for free. I sold five whistles for K5 and the last one I gave away free and one Fox 40 I am keeping for myself since it is the only whistle I need. So I wish to give a big thank you to the national coach at the university in America. Still, I need more whistles and jerseys. I kept four jerseys for myself and I sold two. . . . So I need more jerseys and whistles. This ends the life story. It was written by

Godfried Kolly,
Level 3 Referee in PNG,
East Sepik Province,
Chambri Lakes,
PNG
29/1/96

The type of whistle Godfried so fancied was, in fact, somewhat unusual. It had a rather distinctive sound but, of greater importance, it had a special finger grip such that the referee could continually flourish it on his hand rather than simply wear it on a cord around his neck.[4] Indeed, this whistle was sufficiently unusual for those in Wewak that, we were positive, Godfried did not know it existed, either in name or in nuance of design, until his "first contact" encounter with it.

Significantly, the Fox 40 whistles so instantly and powerfully became an object of crystallized desire for Godfried that their acquisition became – in retrospect – his life work. So intensely was Godfried cathected on the Fox 40s that he could describe himself as not only being pulled through Wewak but through the world more generally. (Cisilia evidently exerted a less enduring, though perhaps comparable, attraction.) Indeed, with the acquisition of the Fox 40s, Godfried felt the fulfillment of his ambitions virtually assured: "I knew that I had become a true referee. All my worries were gone as this is a big part of my life history."

Godfried saw the Fox 40s, thus, as providing his life with both a shape and a trajectory of enrapturing possibility. The Fox 40s would allow him to become a "true referee" in the social field of Wewak, where soccer and other sports periodically engaged more people from disparate cultural groups than any set of endeavors (except, perhaps, church activities). Most of Godfried's non-Chambri acquaintances – those he greeted as he walked through Wewak – were those he knew from sports, particularly from his activities as a "level three" referee. Indeed, his most valued associations outside of the camp were with fellow members of the East Sepik Referees Association.

However, unlike Godfried, most of his fellow referees were, in fact, "shoe-sock" men, men who were actually employed, usually as civil servants. (For example, one worked as a nutritionist for the Provincial Health Department, one as a forester for the Department of Primary Industries, others in various capacities within the Provincial Works Department. These later men we will return to.) These "shoe-sock" men earned lower middle class salaries (at least) and usually occupied government houses located away from the town's ethnic enclaves. (None was a member of Rotary; just one played golf.) They were both motivated and frequently able to shelter (some) income from, and attenuate (some) ties with, their kin. Correspondingly, these men could direct (some of) their social energies and resources toward friendships with their (nonkin) counterparts, often spending evenings buying each other beers at local bars. They could also readily display such lifestyle status markers as decent soccer uniforms, official rule books, homes with electricity and televisions on which they – and their "mates" – could watch soccer matches and other sports events.

It was primarily among these men that Godfried sought respect and acceptance. When he thought that with the arrival of the Fox 40s (and jerseys) his "worries would be gone," he was anticipating recognition from his fellow referees for being a social transactor of significance. He expected they would be as wild for this "trade" as he was. Perhaps to the extent that all other desires became peripheralized, Godfried's "trade" would serve as the fulfillment of desire itself – for them as for him. As he savored what would be his "glory days," Godfried anticipated being the focus of continued admiration and overwhelming desire for what he alone could deliver – and, for what he in a significant sense was. His apotheosis would be to remain, with his Fox 40s, the compelling center of a transactional process: one in which people eagerly bought whistles from him "to make him happy." He wished, in other words, to remain in demand, to remain an object of desire.

Desire's differential promises and risks

The Fox 40 whistles which so entranced Godfried were, we think, at least somewhat comparable in their anticipated effect to those pearl shells (and other trade goods) which so entranced the Highlanders with whom the Leahys transacted. Penambe Tugl recalls his delight when he was first given pearl shells by the Leahys near Mount Hagen:

> I felt as important as the big man! As I was decorating them I was thinking, now I'll be able to make moka! Get married! I could do anything now I have the ultimate! I had a feeling of excitement, of ownership. I put them near my head at night and didn't quite go to sleep, thinking about the shells. Sometimes I'd decorate them and hang them up, and then I'd look at them and admire them. Then I'd sit down and go out, come back and look! And other people would come in and admire them. I just can't explain how I felt about them. I really felt important. (As quoted by Connolly and Anderson, 1987: 129–30)

The sense of excitement and possibility experienced by Penambe Tugl and Godfried do seem partially analogous: each excitedly anticipated that his capacity to shape social relations would be enhanced, whether by effecting compelling transactions of marriage- and *moka*-based kinship and alliance or of soccer-based extra-kin friendships. Yet, if both appeared "wild for the trade" because of the transactional possibilities those objects held, the nature of the objects and the context of their uses had clearly shifted.

The shift was not simply because the pearl shells which the first-contacted Hageners welcomed were significantly familiar whereas the Fox 40s which the more cosmopolitan Godfried coveted were significantly novel. Both items, after all, had value because of their

10. Godfried Kolly resplendent as Chambri cultural performer.

social potency. Rather, the shift was because a world focused on socialities established through prestigious marriage and *moka* payments was crucially different from a world focused on statuses verified through the acquisition of new commodities. Simply put, indigenous valuables and official soccer whistles carried significantly different implications with respect to their acquisition and deployment. The "trade" that Penambe Tugl and his transactors and the "trade" that Godfried and his transactors were "wild for" were differently constituted and thereby carried with them (among other things) different kinds of risks pertaining to different kinds of potential failures. Not only – we will suggest – would Penambe Tugl have a better chance of receiving eminence as a big man in colonial Mount Hagen with introduced pearl shells than would Godfried, as a global trader in postcolonial Wewak with introduced whistles, but failure would in each case create a different kind of person. In one case, failure would mark someone as a person with less influence and power than others; in the other case, failure would mark someone as being the wrong kind of person.

Regardless of whether or not Penambe Tugl succeeded in his aspirations, Godfried's hopes for an apotheotic end to his worries were soon dashed. Scarcely a month after receiving the whistles, Godfried handed the following written (again, translated from the Neo-Melanesian and included here with his permission) lament and rebuke to us when we visited him at the camp. He was again beset by worry. His relationship with his fellow referees had not been significantly transformed by his global traffic. Moreover, his plans to pursue his other major (and related) global interest – that of a world-traveling cultural performer – were also being thwarted. In particular, it seemed unlikely that he (with or without the Yambai Culture Group) would be invited to attend a forthcoming (and widely publicized) Pacific Arts Festival in Apia, Western Samoa.

Note to Deborah Gewertz and Freddy

Yes here I am about to ask the two of you concerning a worry of mine. I am going to give you a big job. If you succeed and I go to Western Samoa, I will be very happy.

(1) I want to say that you haven't helped me or opened one road for me. I have worked for the two of you for a long time and I have seen you help many other Chambri people in the East Sepik Province, but not me

(2) You have helped promote Thomas Sangit but not me.

(3) And you have promoted Walindimi but you have done nothing for my family.

(4) And you have helped many Chambri teachers and businesspeople. . . . At what time have you helped me? I want you to help me by phoning the culture office in Port Moresby today. Thank you my sister Deborah Gewertz. . . .

By Godfried Kolly
Chambri Traditional Man

As we read this letter in Godfried's presence, we found ourselves upset – in fact, hurt (perhaps reacting as others of the middle class when berated for failures of generosity by their grass-roots kin). While, as he had noted, we had helped other Chambri and their enterprises, we had long acknowledged our special and long-term obligations to him. After all, we always paid Godfried a generous fortnightly salary in his guaranteed role as our research assistant (for which he generally had to do no more than be a "traditional anthropologist" engaged in his own ethnographic writings). We frequently gave him and his family gifts of food, clothes and money (both when we were in Papua New Guinea and when we had returned to the United States). And we had brought him the wonderful Fox 40s.

We mentioned these contributions to Godfried, which he readily acknowledged. But he insisted that the help we had given others was different from that we had given him. In the help we had given others, we had opened roads for them along which transactions continued to flow. Thus, we had helped Thomas Sangit – a local craftsmen who received commissions for his carefully carved and painted commemorative plaques – by providing him with promotional photographs of his work so that clients and recognition continued to be drawn to him. We had advertised Walindimi – a men's house in the Chambri Island village of Wombun serving as a tourist site – by describing it in both a brochure and a book so that visitors and recognition continued to be drawn to it. And we had assisted teachers and businesspeople – seeking to enhance their credentials and networks – by writing letters of recommendation for them so that educational and financial opportunities as well as recognition continued to be drawn to them.

But all of Godfried's enterprises had proven to be dead ends. While his fellow referees had been, we think, moderately impressed by the Fox 40s and quite willing to make him "happy" by purchasing them, nothing else seemed to follow. Though they might have been (reasonably) "wild for the trade," Godfried, for his part as global trader, would find it difficult to conclude that he "hadn't done too badly by himself." Like his other ventures, his transactions in Fox 40s had gone nowhere and this meant, he felt, that he had to go somewhere. In particular, he wanted to go to the Pacific Arts Festival in Western Samoa. (This would be his Calgary, his Jayapura.) He needed another shot at becoming the embodiment of the desirable – an embodiment which would demonstrate his capacity to compel those – the members of the middle class – from whom he wished recognition. Going to Western Samoa would constitute double validation – the validation of sponsorship and the validation of cultural embodiment.

As Godfried's essay, "Official Referee Whistle" (and our earlier reference to his activities as president of the Yambai Culture Group), has made clear, he had often sought sponsorship from businesses and parliamentarians. Indeed, we had typed many of his letters requesting sponsorship. Although he never could have gone to Europe or to Western Samoa as "Chambri Traditional Man" without financial endorsement, sponsorship meant more to Godfried than facilitation. For him, impressing sponsors – being accepted by them, being in demand by them – was an end in itself. Moreover, the sponsors he sought were obvious arbiters of lifestyle. They were producers of products connoting affluence, like Pepsi Cola and South Pacific Beer, or they were men enviable by virtue of class position and access to political slush funds, like Somare and Narakobi, politicians in the East Sepik Province.

The "big job" Godfried had for us was to find him a sponsor for the trip to Samoa, much as we had found him one for the whistles and jerseys. In particular, we were to use our networks, especially with the Head of the National Cultural Institute, to insure that he, as profusely decorated and highly skilled cultural performer, could again embody a certain vision of the desirable. An invitation to Apia would demonstrate that he was still in demand, as he was when he had been asked to go to Europe; furthermore, having been to Apia would make him additionally desirable as an agent-emissary for new experiences and products, as he was when he supposedly had scoured seven countries for the Fox 40s.

In other words, he hoped that the trip would work in the same way as the whistles were meant to work, but had not. He hoped the trip would compel middle-class people – sponsors, acquaintances, audiences and associates alike – to recognize his inherent worth as a purveyor. He hoped the trip would compel them to recognize him as an embodiment of the desirable. He wanted both the whistles and the trip to operate as Penambe Tugl had wanted his kina shells to work: to open roads so as to be socially (re)generative. However (and again), the terrain – the socioeconomic ground – these roads were to cross had changed.

The categorical distinctions of colonial life, including those of first-contact encounters, had shifted since the Leahy expedition into the Highlands. The distinctions then allowed James Leahy and his brothers to remain fundamentally detached from the Papua New Guineans among whom they moved and to whom they carried the "trade." In this postcolonial period, it was those of the Papua New Guinea middle class who were cultivating the attitudes and strategies of detachment that would enable them to protect their resources against claims by their less-affluent kin and by acquaintances such as Godfried.

While Penambe Tugl's desire that the wonderful shells from the Leahys would continually augment his reputation – would enhance his intrinsic desirability as they echoed across mountain valleys and generations in bride prices and in *moka* – might have been reasonable, Godfried's comparable desire for his Fox 40 whistles was less so. The legacy left by decades of global trading meant that Godfried's efforts to establish ongoing social efficacy as a "Level 3 Referee in PNG" demanded a lifestyle requiring regular expenditure and, hence, regular income.

Simply and painfully put, as relations of commensurate differences had been increasingly replaced by those of incommensurate differences, there was very little that Godfried could deliver that would attract the continuing attention and interest of those of the middle class, much less gain him the income necessary to join their ranks. As global trader, Godfried was not a success: Fox 40 whistles, although appealing, were not so striking (especially to those who themselves traveled abroad) as to confer lasting celebrity status; nor did their sale provide sufficient profit for further trading enterprises. Most disappointingly, they just did not significantly entail. That his fellow referees bought them to make him happy was simply the small change of a pleasant but finite transaction – the equivalent, perhaps, of a round of drinks at the local hotel.

Thus, in an increasingly class-based Papua New Guinea, Godfried's glory days – his perfect (entrepreneurial) moments – would almost necessarily be of short duration and, hence, ultimately disappointing. Despite his scouring the world for objects of desire, he would, in all probability, remain the wrong person for the right place.

The opened road?

Godfried continued devoting energy towards going to the Pacific Arts Festival. A few months later, he was again filled with excitement. He, with other members of the Yambai Culture Group, had just been commissioned to perform at a local hotel. They were to entertain at a reception hosted by the Public Works Department for the visiting Australian High Commissioner, his party, and an assortment of local and visiting politicians and public servants. The Commissioner was coming to Wewak to open a section of road (between Wewak and the Sepik River town of Angoram) that had been reconstructed and resurfaced with Australian development (AusAid) funds. Many of the government officials to whom Godfried had written for sponsorship would be at the reception. They would see him perform and be so impressed, he was sure, that they would definitely help get him to Western Samoa.

Godfried and the thirty other Chambri involved practiced for days. They would execute six numbers in all. Each would involve different musicians until the final number, when all would perform together. Godfried would be in the first and last numbers, playing the hand drum as well as singing and dancing. Costumes would have to be shared, because there just was not enough shell jewelry in the camp to go around. But the performers would be resplendent, nevertheless – and, as Godfried assured us, the Chambri were the best performers of all Sepik peoples.

It was chilly and rainy throughout the High Commissioner's visit. By the time members of the official party returned to the hotel, they had had a long day. They had first traveled for two hours on rough and slippery surfaces to reach the section of road the Commissioner was to open. Then came the ribbon-cutting, speeches and the lengthy return trip to Wewak. By 6.00 p.m., when they arrived at the hotel reception, most thought they had earned their drinks and dinner. And, of course, there was also the cultural performance to look forward to.

In their turn, the members of the Yambai Culture Group practiced all day at Chambri Camp until around 5.30, when they were transported in a Works' truck to the hotel. There they sought temporary protection from the rain in an open-sided shelter located just outside the area, where the increasingly convivial reception was taking place. Unfortunately, when they were finally asked to leave their shelter to perform outside at about 8.00 p.m. (the Commissioner and his party at that point wanted to wrap things up), the rain had not stopped. Indeed, it had become so torrential that they could complete only half of the planned numbers. They were, nonetheless, thanked heartily by all the dignitaries and were photographed with them by representatives of several newspapers.

The performers were paid less than they had anticipated: rather than the K500 Godfried had expected, only K250 was provided. By the time it became clear that no more money would be forthcoming, the visiting dignitaries had excused themselves and the remaining public servants – including those from Works – were thoroughly drunk. With no one to drive them home, the members of the Yambai Culture Group had to find their soggy way back to the camp on foot. Each member earned only K8 for performing. This would have been enough, if Godfried had ventured, to buy scarcely a couple of drinks at the hotel bar for the fellow soccer referees, employed by Works, who had been at the reception.

Nonetheless, Godfried thought the evening had gone well. He did not, however (and despite our efforts to help), perform in Western Samoa.[5]

5
The problem(s) of the poor

Law, order, tinned mackerel and water buffalo

We have been writing about the complex engagements between rich and poor in a contemporary Papua New Guinea where class distinctions were becoming ever more significant. In the last two chapters we showed in some ethnographic detail how these engagements often perplexed, frustrated and angered those of both the middle class and the grass roots. The middle class certainly expected grass-roots resentment, anticipating that it would lead to smashed windshields at golf functions unless additional security precautions were taken. However, many affluent Papua New Guineans felt that the grass roots posed a far more serious and systematic threat – one to social order itself. Given their amassed resources, whether located in homes or businesses, and their nucleated households, which lacked significant numbers of coresident kin, affluent Papua New Guineans felt chronically vulnerable to criminal attacks. Furthermore, they were concerned that the prospect of such attacks would additionally damage Papua New Guinea's reputation as a place hospitable to business. It was these members of the middle class, in particular, who had begun to utilize a rhetoric of class – both direct and indirect – to describe what was wrong with their society. It was they who often expressed their increasingly preoccupying concerns about the deterioration of law and order in class terms, regarding crime as emanating primarily from the urban grass-roots.

Thus, the president of Port Moresby's Chamber of Commerce and Industry, Minson Peni, said: "A major concern among our members is the law and order issue ... [which] has an adverse effect on both domestic and international investment" (as quoted by Tobia, 1996: 1). The only way, Peni thought, to defeat "the growing monster" of the law and order problem was to create jobs and pass tougher laws. In particular, he supported the passage of a (controversial) Internal Security Act. This was designed to reduce the number of unemployed grass roots living in town by requiring national identity cards and initiating travel restrictions (Tobia, 1996: 1).

Responding to these middle-class concerns, especially those of the business community, (then) Prime Minister Julius Chan had declared 1996 the Year of Law and Order Enforcement.[1] And his efforts were daily endorsed by the country's largest newspaper in a standing inset on its letters and editorial page: "The *Post-Courier* supports PNG Government's Year of Law and Order Enforcement Initiative. Lawbreakers are ruining our nation's image. Every Kina spent on Law and Order is an investment in our nation's future."

Our primary ethnographic focus in this chapter is a law and order rally convened in Wewak. As we will show, in what virtually everyone regarded as a period of turbulent transition, there was a range of opinions offered in speeches by "reasonable" people about how "reasonable" people should act to insure social order. Yet, in part because of the ways the events at this rally were structured, most of the opinions shared certain class implications in common. For instance, plausibility of argument – reasonability of opinion – became defined in a particular way. While ostensibly expressing universalistic concern for the well-being of all Papua New Guineans (as fellow citizens and human beings), these opinions (not surprisingly) constructed and projected into the future a community in which class distinctions became additionally reinforced.

Before describing the rally, we wish to state several provisos. We do not claim that the causes of crime in Papua New Guinea – especially assaults against women – could be entirely explained in class terms, much less fully explained by considering the class aspects in rhetoric about crime. Nor do we claim that our approach here does justice to the pain and fear many Papua New Guineans have felt, *regardless of their class*, as victims of attack. Yet, understanding those Papua New Guinea speeches at the rally is surely to understand something about how crime and class have been conjoined both in fact and in experience. Crime, however brutal, has never simply been a brute fact: its injuries have stemmed, at least in part, from how it has been understood.

We cannot claim, moreover, to approach this topic from a position of neutrality. As should be immediately clear from the anecdote we tell below about our own first robbery, we were sympathetic to the vulnerability of our middle-class friends to robbery and other forms of violence. Certainly, in the many years we have been visiting Papua New Guinea, we never before were so frequently frightened as when we lived in our rented house, behind our padlocked gates, surrounded by the accoutrements of middle-class success.

The rhetoric of crime – of order and disorder

When a friend phoned us about a forthcoming meeting at Wewak's Wirui Catholic Mission concerning ways to "stop the violence" plaguing the town, she knew we were personally involved with law and order issues. (Our friend was a long-term expat and former member of the East Sepik Provincial Assembly.) Our first but not our last personal involvement in law and order had been shortly before the call, when early one morning the padlocks on our gate were cut. Five youths were involved. They came armed with a bolt cutter and bush knives. Their intent was to steal our car. We were not wholly surprised at this predawn intrusion, having talked about criminal activity in Wewak with many middle-class crime victims, both national and expat. However, we were somewhat surprised and certainly disconcerted when no one answered the police emergency line when we called to report the theft-in-progress. (The break-in fortunately was terminated with the smashing of our car window when the youths discovered that not only we, but a security guard, were home.) The friend who phoned us and many other of our middle-class friends wryly told us that if a policeman had answered, he probably would have said that no car was available in which to respond. Or he might have said that the police station could not be left unattended and, hence, itself open to robbery.

All of our middle-class friends – and many of our grass-roots friends – agreed that Wewak (and Papua New Guinea generally) needed more law and order. There was special concern that breaches of law and order often involved violence against women. Indeed, the meeting about which our friend was calling had been precipitated by a particularly egregious attack a few days before: in broad daylight at a crowded market while onlookers stood by, a drunken national grass-roots youth had punched an expat nun repeatedly in the face through her open car window and then simply walked off through the crowd with her stolen handbag. Though the police had been slow to respond, they did apprehend the youth.

However, at least according to rumor, he was too drunk to manage easily so they simply let him go home and sleep it off. Nor were they apparently pursuing the case. Some thought this was because they had been bribed, or were related to the youth. In any case, the youth seemed to have left town, perhaps to hide out in his home village. Such incidents – both the attack and the inadequacy of the police in dealing with it – were intolerable, and the meeting, our friend told us, was to organize an effective public response.

Two such meetings were, in fact, held at the Wirui Mission. Each was well-attended by approximately eighty church-affiliated and community-concerned nationals and expats: priests, nuns, policemen, lawyers, politicians, businessmen, teachers, members of women's advocacy groups. A national woman was selected as chair – indeed, this was the woman with political aspirations whose interest in Mead's *The Mountain Arapesh* we mentioned in chapter 1. She ran the meetings as rather free ranging and heartfelt discussions.

The discussions included passing recognition that crime had both underlying and persisting causes, such as alienation, hunger and unemployment in a lagging economy, and had deleterious long-term implications for investment and tourism. However, the primary focus was on taking immediate steps to stop serious crime against property and persons. This type of crime, as with the assault on the nun, had become endemic to the extent that daily life had lost its reasonability, becoming awfully difficult, if not downright dangerous, for virtually everyone in Papua New Guinea. Certainly the government could not be relied on for action. To accept the many official pronouncements that the government was taking (or soon would take) effective steps would be simply to accept without protest the present levels of personal peril and societal disintegration. The only alternative for dealing with the growing crisis was for concerned citizens to come up promptly with specific plans that could be implemented.

A number of such plans were proposed and endorsed at the meetings: reliable statistics should be collected concerning the number of crimes actually committed in Wewak; policemen should be prohibited from living in squatter settlements, where they might befriend the criminals and tip-off their kin and neighbors; policemen should also be rotated to new areas every two years, so that they could not form excessively close local ties; citizens should be encouraged to become "proactive" and report crime to a well-screened, hot line committee (not to police, who might either ignore

11. The law and order rally began with a procession of some 100 men and women carrying placards calling for an end to fear and violence.

the information or leak the information – and perhaps its source – to the criminals); citizens should also be educated in their responsibilities and legal rights, including the right to make a citizen's arrest; unemployed squatters should be encouraged to leave their settlements and return to their villages; judges should be allowed to commit criminals upon their release from prison to three years residence in their home villages; government officials should implement a general ban on poker machines and alcohol.

However, the most immediate objective should be to stage a rally. This would mobilize public opinion as well as provide the publicity necessary to compel the implementation of the proposed plans. At the rally, senior politicians would be directly confronted with the people's concerns and so would be embarrassed into doing something about them. To this end, a petition would be circulated for signatures at the rally. The petition would then not only be presented to East Sepik's governor, Michael Somare, but subsequently published in the *Post-Courier.* A subcommittee of volunteers and nominees was formed to handle the arrangements for the rally. This subcommittee was composed of five nationals (the chairwoman, a male

12. The parade stopped at a flat-bed truck on which a public address system had been set up.

lawyer, a female teacher, a nun and a female domestic abuse counselor) and one expat (the woman who phoned us).

The rally was scheduled for a Saturday morning, to attract the large crowd convened at the outdoor market on the week's major shopping day. It began with a procession of some 100 men and women – about an equal number of nationals and expats. Included were virtually all who had attended the Wirui Mission meetings. These men and women, carrying placards calling for an end to fear and violence and urging passersby to join them or meet them at the market, were led by a police car with flashing lights. The parade slowly proceeded along the several miles from Wewak's town hall, past the town's principal stores (and under a banner announcing the event) to the main bus stop and outdoor market. At the market, amid the hundreds of those shopping or simply hanging out, the parade stopped at a flat-bed truck on which folding chairs and a public address system had been set up.

Throughout, the event was well-orchestrated, in part because rallies had become common over the years. Indeed, the truck, owned by the local Coca Cola distributor, and the public address system, owned by one of the town's major Chinese wholesalers, generally featured in such events.

In both her initial statement and in her comments during the nearly two-hour rally, the chairwoman set out and reiterated the reasons for the gathering. Speaking primarily in Neo-Melanesian, as did the other speakers, she reminded listeners of the many problems affecting all members of the community. She especially stressed those directed against women by young criminals. It was these men who snatched purses, who stole money from women selling produce at the market and who maliciously – for no reason at all – ruined their wares by trampling or spitting on them. These criminals did nothing but smoke marijuana and get drunk, rob shops and break into houses, beat their wives, assault other women, even nuns. People, she said, are sick and tired of this. They want to walk about freely. All must cooperate to get rid of such men. Leading the crowd in call and response she cried out: "Don't you want Wewak to become paradise?" "Yes," from the crowd. "Don't you want freedom?" "Yes." "Don't you want justice?" "Don't you want a good life with your family?" "Well, this is what we must all work for." She then read out the petition[2] and sent copies of it into the crowd for signatures. (The copies were conveyed by noticeably burly no-nonsense men – presumably to ensure their safe return and to provide indirect testimony that these men opposed violence against women.) Not one of the senior politicians in the East Sepik Province came to the rally and their absence was understood as all-too-predictable. Governor Somare was away in Cyprus and Deputy Governor Anisi was not able to attend. Consequently, the petition bearing signatures would be presented to the acting police commander.

Collectively, the fifteen speakers the chairwoman introduced during the rally presented what we had come to recognize as a familiar range (and sometimes mixture) of plausible ideas concerning the nature of social order and disorder: concerning how reasonable human beings should and should not live together. Of the twelve speakers selected in advance, only some had attended the Wirui Mission meetings. Others were asked because of their stature as community leaders. In addition, three came forward from the audience, asking to speak.

What then were the Papua New Guinean speeches about? How was crime being understood (and experienced)?

Three speakers had primarily a religious perspective. These were all national males: a Seventh Day Adventist pastor and two self-identified "grass-roots youth" who were active in Antioch, a Catholic youth-focused revival movement (see Gewertz and Errington, 1996). The pastor laid the blame on Lucifer for ruining everyday life in the East Sepik. (Lucifer, it seemed, had twenty-three names – including two well known in Sepik mythology, those of Segundimi and Mongoiyebi.) All three agreed that Satan, in his various guises, could truly be defeated only by Jesus – not by the government or by the law alone. As one of the youth put it: "Without Jesus' wisdom, nothing will control us. I know that hell waits for those who sin. The fear of the Lord is the beginning of all wisdom and understanding."

Three speakers, all nationals, had primarily a family values perspective – though one which took a religious turn. They were a Catholic priest, a nun and a male former politician. The Father appealed to everyone in town to work on his or her own behalf, since waiting for Michael Somare or Julius Chan to do something would be futile. He continued: "We are all Christians – no one here is heathen. We must start with the children, teaching them about God. They shouldn't be beaten but should be disciplined. Fathers and mothers must teach their children to respect others." The nun agreed, especially enjoining parents to set good examples for their children by not buying stolen goods. "Don't you think," she asked, "that your children know when you do wrong? You must remember that it is they who will be the leaders of the future." Moreover, she said: "In villages people take action if there is violence. Why can't we do the same here in town?" The former politician (who had come forward on his own) berated Somare and others for not attending the rally and for neglecting local concerns. He then asked how the future might be made better for children. He suggested a lesson to be learned from his own family circumstances. His father had been a policeman who (like Somare) was always away from home trying to solve the problems of others. But he did nothing to guide his own family, and now many of his children have problems. Parents must work hard to teach their children about God and to provide them with the necessities they need. Politicians will not do this.

Two speakers had a primarily civic perspective. One was a national male lawyer and the other, the expat woman who notified us of the first Wirui Mission meeting. The lawyer admitted that he felt guilty when first asked to attend the Wirui Mission meeting, "because in the courtroom I try my best to free my criminals." But, he also knew that it was somewhat the public's fault for making his job easy and for not doing more to combat crime more generally: people did not help policemen gather evidence, much less find criminals – nor did they testify in court or make citizen's arrests. The expat woman bemoaned the prevalence of those who had no interest in Wewak – those who allowed it to remain dirty, strewn with broken glass and other litter; those who continued to spit betel nut juice on the streets. Moreover, the town council would do nothing to deal with this situation unless the good citizens of Wewak opened their mouths and insisted that civil servants do their jobs. If the people wished for law and order, then they must do something about it: they must take to heart the Chinese proverb that "If every man cleans his own doorstep, the whole world will be clean."

Three speakers had a primarily traditionalist perspective. All were national men – a lawyer, a self-identified "elder" and a politician. The lawyer said that the East Sepik could indeed be paradise – if people were not so lazy, just hanging around, doing nothing in town. Everybody in town without jobs should go back to their villages where they could support themselves by working their own land. The elder (who had come forward on his own) thought that people should return home as well as eschew nontraditional practices. He lamented the fact that young Papua New Guineans were interested only in the accoutrements and customs of white culture and white men. One young high school student, for example, modeled himself on Rambo. One night he got drunk, took a chain saw and began destroying another man's fence. In trying to stop him, neighbors injured him rather badly. While rushing him to the hospital in their car, they crashed and he was killed. The speaker concluded: "So much for Rambo's power – so much for the power of the white man. The root cause of the law and order problem is that we have lost our traditions. Yet, here we are speaking to one another on top of a Coca Cola truck when we should really stop all advertising and ban all videos. That's where our youth learn about evil ways. They learn to say things to me like 'you ashole.' I tell you they must go back and listen to their fathers and mothers in their villages."

The politician (who had also come forward on his own) added a distinctly autocratic twist to his traditionalist perspective. He blamed lawyers (including those present) for providing Papua New Guineans, especially women, with too much freedom. The constitution brought a democracy which abnegated traditional patriarchal authority. No longer were "our fathers, the bosses." No longer were male elders able to discipline out-of-control sons and daughters. To rectify this, "the lawyers must take the lead in curtailing our freedoms before the year 2000." Freedom of movement should be minimized. Everyone should wear name tags (perhaps a reference to the previously mentioned Internal Security Act). Freedom has "overridden our customary orientations." Addressing the women present, he warned them that they were themselves likely responsible for domestic violence because they angered husbands when they "step over the marks" (English phrase used).

Two speakers, both national women, had primarily a feminist perspective. One, a domestic abuse counselor working for the East Sepik Council of Women, waited for no introduction. She grabbed the microphone from the autocratic traditionalist, demanding to know what he meant by the phrase, "step over the marks": "Whose marks? Are you the god of us all? I am telling you that all human beings have rights. And we are here to fight for women's rights, mother's rights and children's rights. We are all individual human beings and everyone has rights to freedom and justice." The other woman, the owner of a local guest house (mentioned in chapter 2 as a SWIT organizer), had spoken earlier. She had appealed to the reasonability of the men in the audience by reminding them that they all had mothers – that none of them would be sitting there, chewing betel nut and listening to the speakers, if not for a woman. She elaborated: "You should feel ashamed when you rape women and steal from them. These aren't the behaviors of human beings. They are the behaviors of animals – of cows, pigs and chickens. I saw a man at the market urinating on a car; a woman objected and he began to curse her. He should have been ashamed. He was once a child. He sucked at his mother's breast. In each one of our families, we must teach our children to respect all human beings. Only then will our communities and countries grow strong. Then we will have justice and be free."

One speaker had a primarily sociological perspective. He was a national male, the coordinator of a criminal rehabilitation program. After congratulating the rally's organizers for creating a forum so that people might speak about their mutual concerns and hardships, he said that all must also realize that "there is a system of injustice at work within the Province." Although human beings must certainly have their needs met – physical, emotional, mental and spiritual – and parents must teach their children, there was more to the law and order issue than this: "Law and order is a game played between the rich and the poor. Frustration builds up among poor people who then want to bring others down to their level. Since it is injustice that causes frustration, law and order is more than a problem of youth. We have to blame the system."

Finally, the acting police commander (virtually by definition, a national male) spoke in his official capacity: "All throughout Wewak, people are being attacked. Much of this violence is directed against women, probably because women can't easily fight back. It is a big problem and everyone must help the police. The law and order problem in this town is not just the problem of the police. It also is the problem of communities. Members of the community must not hide criminals. Families within communities must educate children to respect law and order. This is why I am pleased to launch this law and order campaign and accept these petitions on behalf of the government."

The chairwoman then presented the signed petitions to the acting police commander and thanked both speakers and audience for their support. Finally, she called again upon the Catholic Father (who had spoken earlier) to close the rally with a prayer. After thanking Coca Cola and the wholesaler for the truck and amplifying system and those who had organized, attended, and spoken in the rally, he enjoined us all to "praise God, three-one [the Trinity], for making us reasonable human beings capable of respecting one another."

The organizers of the rally were pleased with its immediate effect. They thought it had been compelling. And although many did attend to their shopping and although the buses were full (service had not been interrupted as the chairwoman had requested), hundreds had listened intently. Certainly the event had gone smoothly. Speakers kept generally on topic and on time. The chairwoman provided often engaging transitions between speakers, sometimes offering supplemental examples to reinforce points just made. Thus, after the nun spoke concerning the vital importance of properly socializing one's children, the chairwoman reminded the audience of a shocking and relatively recent incident (the virtual antithesis of reasonable behavior): a young settlement dweller was said to have struck and killed his mother when she did not give him the 20 toea (about US$.16) he demanded to buy several cigarettes. In addition, audience interest was maintained by lively musical interludes provided by a grass-roots band of young men and women from one of Wewak's squatter settlements. These performed such songs concerning issues of law and order as "The Law Prohibits Hitting Women"[3] and "Equality, Development and Peace."

And, of course, as many speakers stressed, the topic of the rally, focused as it was on law and order problems as they played out largely in violence against women, was of broad concern. There appeared to be a clear attempt by rally organizers to unite Wewak residents, whether of the grass-roots poor or affluent middle class, in a Durkheimian sociality generated in response to deviance – to an affront against (what were presented as) ontological social values. Because – as any reasonable person should recognize – all had mothers, sisters and daughters who were subject to attack, and because all had been born of and suckled by women, all could unite in deep concern about women's vulnerability if not actual injury.

Moreover, it seemed to us that the Durkheimian nature of this community was additionally orchestrated to downplay the divisive significance of class (and other, such as, ethnic) distinctions. The ostensibly inclusive range of plausible perspectives (religious, family values, civic, traditionalist, feminist, sociological and official), given by an ostensibly inclusive range of social actors (middle-class professionals, grass-roots urban youth and village elders), invoked the existence of an organically solidary, comprehensive community on a liberal democratic model of reasonability. This was a community in which all participants – all voices and perspectives – were equally valued in that all should be heard. Even the brief clash between the autocratic traditionalist and the feminist could be regarded as the democratic exchange of different ideas necessary to forge a genuinely shared sociality.

However, while the form of the rally itself asserted that society had (or should have) a particular form, one in which all men and women could in their various differences equally participate, the form of the rally *also* limited the degree to which those "differences that make a difference" in actual society could be expressed and confronted. Each speaker was not only limited to the same relatively brief amount of time, but each had to acknowledge that the other speakers and their perspectives were equally plausible and worthy of a hearing: in short, perspectives could be aired, but not really argued. Hence, the virtual requirement that each must respect the others' opinions meant that there was little opportunity for a critical edge.[4] Indeed, to present such an edge would have challenged the rally's hard-won ethos of mutual respect in a search for shared ontological values.[5]

The only speaker to present any significant challenge to the rally's claim that all were equally in this together was the coordinator of the criminal rehabilitation program. His sociological perspective concerning social injustice and frustration generated by the differences between the rich and the poor might, if carried further, have provided the critical edge that was lacking.[6] He, in effect, was the only one to argue that crime was not an unreasonable, inappropriate response to contemporary Papua New Guinean socioeconomic circumstances. Even he, however, had to acknowledge the value of the forum and the validity of the other perspectives. If he had not, he would have, in effect, declared himself asocial and, therefore, irrelevant. In this context, his perspective – which, again, could really only be aired and not argued – became simply one of several equally weighted perspectives.

However, in our view, the fundamental equality of condition the rally sought to project on Wewak was as *faux* with respect to actual political realities as SWIT's rhetoric was with respect to actual economic ones. Thus, perhaps appropriately, the rally, as a kind of free market of ideas (offered on top of a Coca Cola truck through the use of a wholesaler's public address system), took place at the same marketplace where the poor women of Wewak (called upon by the rally to unite with middle-class women as "women") continued to sit long hours selling their crafts (having failed to work hard enough to make it to Jayapura). In both cases – that of the rally and of SWIT – the projected image of society disguised the huge and, in a class system, inherent inequality actually in existence.

In fact, implicit in the rally's denial that Papua New Guineans were fundamentally separated by class distinctions with respect to issues of law and order (again, all suffered from crime, all should respect women as the source of human life and nurture) was the affirmation of a common middle-class assumption about the significance of class distinctions. In ways that echoed SWIT's rhetoric about poverty as personal failure, the rally's rhetoric strongly suggested that members of the grass-roots were, through their individual failings – their incapacity to make socially appropriate choices – primarily responsible for crime. They were responsible even for the crime besetting and disfiguring their own grass-roots lives (in a variant of "blaming the victim"). Thus, if law and order problems were the result of poor socialization such that most criminals were grass-roots youths (like the one who killed his mother and the one who attacked the nun), then the problem of law and order derived primarily from the failure of grass-roots parents to maintain and transmit the proper Christian family values necessary to keep Lucifer at bay and teach respect for others. Hence, crime was primarily the fault of the grass-roots. Moreover (to pick up another rhetorical thread), if urban grass roots families could not properly socialize their children, then they should all go back to their villages. There, family authority would be bolstered by tradition such that youth could be adequately controlled. In any case, such youth would no longer trouble either those of the grass roots remaining in town as productive members of the labor force or the members of the (largely urban) middle class.

Correspondingly no one at the rally talked about the exigencies of squatter life, or about how those exigencies might be satisfactorily met. Indeed, in our experience, few of the middle class ever talked about such matters. This was presumably consistent with their emphasis on sheltering their resources from extended kin so as to consume within their nucleated families. (Even the rehabilitation coordinator, whom we interviewed at length, shared this middle-class strategy.) Further, although many of the middle class favored sending the grass roots back to home villages, few thought much about how alienating life there would be for urban grass-roots youth. Many of these had been born in town; for them (as, in different ways, for those of the middle class), the home village was not home at all. In addition, few of those who proposed a return to villages realized that those returning might not be welcomed. In some villages, land might already be scarce because of population growth and cash-cropping. And villagers were unlikely to welcome those they considered likely to engage in crime and incivility – including addressing elders as "assholes." Finally, few (excepting some, like the domestic abuse counselor) were willing to admit the extent to which members of the middle class contributed to law and order problems. Entitled, bored and destructive youth as well as corrupt, drunken and violent husbands were far from unknown in the middle class.[7]

When we returned home that afternoon from the rally – having in fact been (somewhat) caught up in its Durkheimian communitas of the right-minded together in social solidary – we noted something wrong. As we unlocked our gate to drive into the compound, we saw that the side door to our house was askew. While we had been listening to the acting police commander and others (and as our security guard attended a Seventh Day Adventist service), the door had been pried open. Stolen were two large suitcases in which the thieves had carried away our possessions. What was missing, as we later reported to the police (who did come to our assistance, this time), were a fair number of goods (but not, in fact, more than those owned by many of our middle-class friends): two cameras, three tape recorders, a compact-disc player, two speakers, a stainless steel folding knife, a short-wave portable radio, two carry-on leather-trimmed suitcases, a pair of men's running shoes, a pocket calculator, a portable computer printer, twenty assorted compact disks (including Bob Dylan!!), two pairs of men's jeans, seven men's polo shirts, two pairs of men's hiking shorts, a traveling clock, two flashlights, two towels, one piece of wrap-around cloth (a "laplap"), an unopened bottle of whiskey, four packs of shortbread biscuits, five large chocolate bars, three lithium camera batteries, and a carton of AA batteries. Fortunately, they could not readily carry away our desk-top computer or our television.

Our Chambri friends living in the squatter settlement, while sympathetic and volunteering to pursue their own grass-roots networks for information, thought our theft was an entirely predictable result: it would not have happened if we had been living among them, as we had in the past. From what nearby squatter settlement, all of us – we, the police and the Chambri – found ourselves wondering, had the thieves come?

Other talk

Father Cherobim Dambui, acting bishop of Wewak and former premier of the East Sepik Province, frequently thought about law and order problems in Papua New Guinea – in part because the church premises and personnel under his direct care were so frequently attacked and robbed. As he reflected to us:

> There is an ideal held up, but very few can achieve it. For the very top people of the country, the ideal is like that of their counterparts elsewhere in the world. The homes, gardens and schools they want are like those wanted elsewhere. At the middle managerial level, people also aspire to what they see as this same kind of better life. What they imitate though is not achievable by most other Papua New Guineans. . . .
>
> Our educational system has been designed for labor recruiting, but there are few jobs now. We have not been educating for life in the villages. The bulk of the people live in rural areas and have no money. They know that the cream of the people live in the towns and that

money is in the towns. So what inevitably happens? People in rural areas come to towns. Our country has not addressed the problem of rural drift. There could be more options for rural areas. But we have been conditioned to channel money to towns. That's where hospitals are; that's where the administrative buildings are; that's where those who make decisions live. That the money will continue to go to the towns is predestined, given the economy. ... The clerks will have to be paid; the public servants will have to be paid. And the money they are paid will be recycled through the stores in the towns and so the towns will continue to grow.

Papua New Guinea towns today are in a makeshift situation. People just smash bottles on the street and don't care. They spit betel nut everywhere and don't care. There is a transient feeling. This is not our place, most people think. They feel that they are just passing through.

The wholesaler who had supplied the public address system at the rally posed a question to the National Minister for Commerce and Industry during the minister's meeting with members of the Sepik Chamber of Commerce and Industry in Wewak. At the question and answer session (following drinks and preceding dinner), the wholesaler asked the minister to explain the 100 percent duty on imported, tinned mackerel – the staple protein of the urban grass roots. The wholesaler felt that "the grass-roots people have been suffering" because of the exorbitantly high tariff. The minister immediately turned the question over to his permanent secretary:

THE SECRETARY: Concerning mackerel, we agree that it has become expensive. But the cost is tied to the economy as a whole. There was a serious developer who wished to create a can-making and fish-processing facility. To encourage his investing in the country, he was promised a total ban on imported mackerel. This was then reduced to a 100 percent tariff. We can't renege on the promise which is a matter of law now. ... We are bound by our promise for five years – there are three more to go.

THE WHOLESALER: You are saying it is unlikely we will get any reduction in the tariff to allow us to lower the price of mackerel. Can you get the company to lower its own price [so that its mackerel sells for less than the duty-inflated imports]?

THE SECRETARY: The company won't agree even if the government wants it to, and why should it? It has had to borrow money as any other business does. We promised the tariff to it. We can't renege; inconsistent government policies will frighten away investors. I am afraid we may not be able to satisfy consumers until the five years are over.

> THE WHOLESALER: How are you going to explain this to people whose incomes have been reduced [through recent devaluation of the kina]? One day their staple food costs 80t; the next day it costs K2. Where do people come in?
> THE SECRETARY: We are aware of these concerns but the agreement was legally signed. It may have been a bad decision, but we are now left with the problem. It is like a marriage. You just can't divorce your wife easily.
> THE WHOLESALER: It is a big concern for us ... There are 3.5 million people in the country and they are being sacrificed so that 400 to 500 can be employed. The International Foods Corporation is making a fortune: 50 million kina a year. To stay in business, we as traders want affordable prices on quality goods.

A young Chambri friend, who belonged to the same Catholic youth organization as did the grass-roots youth who spoke at the rally, wrote the following stylized autobiographical account concerning his criminal past. We translate from Neo-Melanesian:

> During my teenage stage I was lost and confused concerning my life. I wasn't clear about what life means for a person born on the earth.
>
> When I saw the educated and rich people enjoying their lifestyles, I envied them. I wanted to become like them, but I felt that I wasn't good enough. There was only one way, I thought, and that was to join a secret gang ... and steal possessions and money from others. It was in this way, I thought, that I could fulfill my dreams and become special.
>
> One time, I met with two cousins of mine on my father's side of the family and a cousin on my mother's side of the family. I met with them to form a little secret gang ... As gang members, we snuck out at night [without our parents knowing] to steal things belonging to other people, sometimes by making them put their hands up as we stole their money.
>
> It wasn't too long before some fellow Chambri and some other friends learned about this little gang of ours. They wanted to join us and before long there were many people in it, almost all the young men in the settlement. During the nights and the days we went around to engage in all sorts of criminal activity throughout the Wewak town area.
>
> After about a year, the men and women of our community became aware of the secret gang. The elders of the community were angry and there was a lot of talk about how to stop us. Many members of the community hated us and gossiped about us. Some of our members, upon hearing the angry talk of the elders, gave up the gang. I and some others, however, did not give up but continued. ...

> Once, after stealing from a store, we were running away when the police caught us and locked us up. We were convicted and sent to the Boram Correctional Institute ... Inside the jail, I sat down and waited and thought hard and worried ... I felt that I had become a slave at hard labor with no freedom to do anything I liked.
>
> Every week on Friday, a pastor of the United Church came to the jail to preach to us. Once, I went and sat down and heard him speak about things I felt were true and good. Man, I thought, his talk really helps me to clarify my thinking. One talk in particular touched me and helped me a lot: "If you are in the jail of sin, come to Jesus and he will set you free. Never mind if you have done very bad things and if you have turned your back on him. Even so, Jesus loves you." When the pastor said these word, I thought to myself, this pastor is talking to me directly.
>
> During the night as I was in my bed, I thought about the pastor's talk. I prayed to God: "Father, help me give up my bad habits and change my bad ways" ... Eventually, my prayers were answered.

Bernard Narakobi, after writing *The Melanesian Way*, was widely rumored to have acquired considerable wealth in the course of his long political career – enough, for instance, to have his numerous children educated abroad. We met him at a meeting in Wewak where, as Wewak's Member of the National Parliament, he was explaining new governmental policies (including the "structural adjustments" imposed by the World Bank and IMF). In describing forthcoming stringencies, he said that villagers should no longer aspire to Toyota Land Cruisers; instead of holding these unreasonable expectations, they should be content with "appropriate technology" such as water buffalo. Following the meeting, he was driven away in a new Land Cruiser.

We were again robbed while we were out one day. Subsequently, bars were put on our doors and windows and an additional security person was hired.

6
Class and the definition of reasonability

The case of the "compo girl"

As we have been showing throughout this book, members of the affluent middle class – bureaucrats, professionals, politicians and businesspeople – had become committed to changing the nature of distinction. Consistent with achieving the "homes, gardens and schools" referred to by Father Dambui in the last chapter, they were promulgating a reclassification of identities and interests: they were reclassifying people as to their worth and their prospects. Thus, the words they used to describe crime and class said, in effect, that certain Papua New Guineans (the poorly socialized of the urban grass roots) were no longer able to make socially appropriate – reasonable – choices.

In this chapter we continue to examine the changing nature and basis of "reasonability." We do so to learn how middle-class Papua New Guineans have been increasingly able to associate themselves with – reasonable – middle-class people wherever they might be and to dissociate themselves from many of their fellow – unreasonable – countrymen. (Such a dissociation was, of course, necessary if Papua New Guinean golfers were to snap their fingers at Papua New Guinean caddies, to return to an earlier example.) Our concentration is, therefore, in this final ethnographic chapter somewhat broader than in the others. Here we move beyond Wewak to understand how class distinctions have come in a nearly absolute sense to separate some who were living modern, relatively individualistic, lives from many who were living more traditional, more collectively oriented, lives. In the case we examine, matters of gender, especially as they related to the self-determination of women as modern individuals with constitutional rights, came to facilitate this separation.

The gendered story of class distinction we tell focuses on the "compo girl," whose (genuine) travails first became widely known on 3 May 1996. On that day the *Post-Courier*, Papua New Guinea's English-language newspaper with the largest circulation, published a front-page story about her. Directly under a lead headline, "Girl Sold in Death Compo," was the following sentence: "A young girl has been included as part of a compensation payment to the relatives of one of two men shot dead by police recently" (Palme, 1996a: 1). According to the article, on April 12th, the police had killed Robert Mond and Koidam Willingal in an early morning attack at their home village near Minj, Western Highlands Province. Mond, a former policeman, was wanted for "holding up policemen in a police station raid, stealing firearms, raping women and many other crimes"; Willingal was believed to be his "bodyguard" (Palme, 1996a: 1). While not contesting that Mond's criminality might have provoked his death at police hands, villagers strongly denied that Willingal was an appropriate police target. They rejected the police claim that he was in league with Mond. Indeed, it was in partial compensation for Willingal's unjustified death at police hands that the compo girl was featured. She was to be in lieu of K20,000. (Twenty-four pigs were also part of the compensation.)

To judge by the reactions of many of the middle class we knew – both nationals and expats – the article was indeed, newsworthy, absorbing their attention and, likely, that of much of the paper's largely middle-class readership (of, in 1995, approximately 41,000).[1] As the case about the constitutionality of such compensation payments developed in the courts of public opinion as well as of national law, it clearly engaged their concerns about how the national community (or perhaps more accurately, communities) of Papua New Guinea should be formed.

As we shall see, the case of the compo girl provided the middle class in Papua New Guinea and beyond – the case was, for instance, featured in the *New York Times* (Mydans, 1997c)[2] – with a vivid context for exploring what were worldwide and intersecting preoccupations about constituting a contemporary social ontology: in particular, about determining the nature of, and articulation between, culture, class, gender and nation. As others have made clear in studies of Pacific elites (Hau'ofa, 1987; Hooper and Huntsman, 1990; Foster, 1992, 1995; Jacobsen, 1995; Keesing, 1996), these preoccupations demanded working through – often contending about – the appropriate relationships between tradition, modernity, choice and social distinction. As the subject of speculation in conversation, in the press and in the court, the case of the compo girl was an evident working through of these relationships. Indeed, in many senses, it was a morality play in which the players embodied these characteristics of tradition, modernity, choice and social distinction. In so doing, they provided to Papua New Guineans and others worldwide a human drama of broad interest about the creation of contemporary sociality itself.

That this Papua New Guinean morality play dealt with such widely held preoccupations was, of course, itself partly the product of worldwide processes, such as the effects of global capital (see Friedman, 1992), in delineating the critical parameters of contemporary social ontologies. That these preoccupations were widely held did not, however, preclude that they were also locally shaped. The same was true concerning ethnic discord in mineral-rich African states, affirmative action and welfare reform in America, clitoridectomies in France. But, as with these other instances, the Papua New Guinea compo girl case could be taken as (perhaps, morally) instructive for both Papua New Guineans and the rest of us about how, and in whose interests, social ontologies were being (re)configured in a contemporary world.

Central to the wrangles engaging Papua New Guineans in their efforts to shape a viable social ontology for their nation was, as we have already suggested, the exploration of gender under conditions both of tradition and of modernity. Discussion and adjudication of the gender issues in the compo girl case by largely middle-class Papua New Guineans became a context, if not a vehicle, for the transformation of the ostensible coequality of the country's many diverse traditions into the subordination of tradition in general by class. By opening tradition to the "enlightened" appraisal of the modern and educated (those of the middle class), certain customs – especially pertaining to gender – were revealed as benighted. In so doing, the intervention by members of the middle class in the compo girl case affirmed an assumed principle that they were in a position to review and judge those leading traditional lives. It also effected the compo girl's release from the constraint of such customs into the modern world in which she could pursue her own choices – her own initiatives and dreams. Thus, those of the middle class were implementing what might be viewed as a postcolonial variant of indirect rule – the epistemological subordination of those leading traditional lives. We think they were in so doing replacing the revealed injuries of tradition with the hidden injuries of class.

Discussion at a Mount Hagen Lodge

In the court of public opinion, it was hard to imagine a more appropriately select and engaged company to discuss the case than the one we happened across near Mount Hagen, the provincial capital of the Western Highlands, on the evening of May 27th. The case of the compo girl was about to be brought before national court there. She proved to be an eighteen-year-old named Miriam Willingal. We will refer to her simply as Miriam to distinguish her from her father. The court would be asked to issue an injunction to prevent her transfer in compensation until the constitutionality of such a transfer could be determined. The court was also being asked to place her in protective custody until a final decision was reached.

We were staying at a guest lodge built largely of traditional materials but provided with modern conveniences. At the lodge we met Patricia Thompson, the proprietor and a Papua New Guinean of considerable distinction. She was a businesswoman and filmmaker, and was married to an expat accountant. Their three children were receiving expensive educations: two at the International Schools in Port Moresby and Mount Hagen and one, in England. She also had an interesting background. Her father was one of several well-known brothers, among the first whites to explore the Highlands. These brothers had sired by local women a number of children, including Thompson.

Richard Chambers, Thompson's nephew, was also at the lodge as someone who had simply stopped by for a chat. He was the grandson of another of these brothers and an accountant for a Mount Hagen transport service. (His very elaborate "traditional" wedding was featured in *Stolen Moments*, Thompson's film of middle-class life in Mount Hagen, about which we will say more below.)

In addition, two Papua New Guineans to figure in the evening's conversation had come to the lodge for dinner. One was Susan Balen, a young lawyer, originally from the Enga Province. Susan was employed by Individual and Community Rights Advocacy Forum (ICRAF), a Port Moresby human rights organization. She was in Mount Hagen to argue for Miriam's protective custody. (It had been ICRAF's initiative, in response to a second *Post-Courier* article of May 9th reporting Miriam as "torn between her desires, ambitions, her person and the tribal obligations and commitment to the traditional practices she no longer believes in" [Palme, 1996b: 2], that had brought the compo girl case to court.) Balen (also her husband, a lawyer from Enga) was clearly of the middle-class professional elite. Her two children, for instance, attended an International School in Port Moresby. Yet as the first "fully educated" member of her family, Balen wanted them to be comfortable in Enga, even as she prepared them for successful careers. She believed the village was "a fine place to live," although many of those living there were "lazy" and "wasting their time." To make them comfortable in Enga, she made a point of feeding them native foods. Yet, she admitted that when they visited their grandparents in the village, they sorely missed their television and computer games.

The other Papua New Guinean who had come for dinner was Father Robert Lak, a priest from the Mount Hagen area who held a local parish. Although some of his parishioners thought that a priest should limit his concerns to religious matters, he planned to run for Parliament during the next election (against Pius Wingti, a former prime minister), believing that the country needed "Christian leadership." (Lak was, in fact, subsequently elected.) It was into his protective custody that Balen hoped Miriam might be placed until her legal rights could be clarified.

Our discussion of the compo girl case began over drinks, continued during dinner at the common dining table and then went on, well into the night, around the central fire in the main public area of the lodge. It was a fascinating evening. Having made clear our long-term anthropological interests in a changing Papua New Guinea, we mostly just listened. Of course we wanted to know more about the facts of the case, but we were especially interested in how these educated, thoughtful and articulate Papua New Guineans viewed its legal, and more broadly social, implications.

Balen, who was to present her argument in court the following day, rehearsed her understanding of the circumstances of the case. In preparing her case, she had consulted with Dr. John Muke, an archeologist (on sick leave from his teaching position in the Sociology–Anthropology Department at the University of Papua New Guinea). He was a member of Willingal's patriclan and had been in the area when the events unfolded. While Balen acknowledged that there were still many ethnographic details about Minj culture she did not fully understand, she felt she was clear on the general picture. Two clans were involved: Willingal's mother's clan and Willingal's own clan. Those of the mother's clan were claiming a "head payment" from members of Willingal's clan. This claim was being made under somewhat unusual circumstances. In particular, Willingal's two wives and five children (including Miriam) were, and for a long time had been, living on tribal land belonging to the mother's clan. They were there as refugees; tribal war had made living on Willingal's land unsafe. Nevertheless, Willingal remained on his land to protect it. Moreover, the head payment was to compensate members of the mother's clan for the death of Willingal (their maternal nephew) at the hands of the police at the time they had pursued and killed Robert Mond. The mother's clan contended that Willingal's clansmen had not cared enough for the deceased Willingal to keep him from being killed. Yet, it would have been very difficult for them to have protected him. Indeed, no one even knew he was a police target. He was unarmed and unresisting and the police shot him well after they had killed Mond. (All of the Papua New Guineans listening to Balen's account agreed that police excess was common and contributed other accounts.)

Willingal's maternal clansmen had initially wanted K20,000 and 600 pigs, or two marriageable women. But they would settle for less money, fewer pigs and one woman. Miriam was the only marriageable woman available, and so Willingal's clan – her clan, as well – included her as central to the head payment they acknowledged owing. The clan, Balen thought, was in a terrible bind, as many of its members were living on the land of those demanding compensation from them – as were Willingal's own family. Therefore, none of them felt in a position to contest the claim against them for compensation. All parties agreed to the terms – even Miriam – and so the case had been settled. Or so it seemed until ICRAF intervened and petitioned a judge to hear her case. ICRAF argued that, regardless of local custom, trading in women could not be allowed because it was a violation of fundamental human rights. Moreover, such compensation demands were obviously not in Miriam's particular interests: she was only eighteen and had hoped to complete her education. (She had been working through a distance education program to improve her Grade Ten examination results sufficiently so that she might enter secretarial school.) She wanted eventually to get a job and have financial independence. ICRAF contended that she should have been allowed to pursue her aspirations.

To be sure, Miriam had initially acceded to the wishes of her elders, but that was largely out of concern for her younger sisters and other younger clanswomen, who might be sought if she refused. She tried to think of the compensation as an arranged marriage. But she did not want this, especially since she did not even know to whom she might be married, no particular man having been designated. (The *Post-Courier*, in describing ICRAF's interest in the case, wrote that Miriam "did not know who she was supposed to marry, his age, interests, personality and other attributes a young woman would look for in a man before marrying her lifetime partner" [Palme, 1996b: 2].) Indeed, Balen was convinced that the young men of the group were not viewing the compensation as an arranged marriage at all: they viewed it as an invitation to rape or in other ways abuse Miriam sexually. Young men today, she said, "are not reliable." (Indeed, she mentioned that she did not fully trust her own brothers, whom she had threatened with court if they ever abused their wives.) Regardless, the world had already changed sufficiently so as to make such compensations, by their very nature, an abrogation of human rights.

Richard Chambers and Patricia Thompson took a somewhat broader perspective than Balen, though they too found the case troubling. Chambers was not convinced that important customs should be looked at primarily from the perspective of individual rights. Elders were, in fact, generally "wise" and the head payments they valued were probably "good." Such payments were, likely as not, of overall benefit because they "ensured peace and unity."

Agreeing with Chambers' general position, Thompson began to address particulars of this case, suggesting that they might be more complex than Balen realized. For instance, Thompson was not at all sure that Miriam faced likely sexual abuse if given in what was, after all, a traditional compensation – that of head payment. Although in traditional Highlands' cultures, women might be sexually assaulted as part of intergroup hostilities (as when they were raped during warfare), sexual assault in this case seemed unlikely since head payments were acts of peace, not of war. Moreover, she wondered who was to determine what was an arranged marriage and what was not: the line between a marriage based on arrangement and on personal choice was often a fine one. Thus, as was often the case, if aunts or other kin told you that such and such a match would be good for the entire clan, you were likely to take them seriously and willingly accept the marriage. (Certainly, we might add, some of the Papua New Guinean mothers of her explorer-descended kin had acceded to family pressures in entering into relationships of political and economic advantage to their relatives [see Connolly and Anderson, 1987].) And bride prices, because they cemented such clan-benefiting matches, were not necessarily a bad thing either. (Indeed, Thompson had mentioned to us that she often found herself caught up in her own clan's affinal and other transactions, sometimes acting like a "barbarian" in her identification with her clan's interests, including success in inter-group competition.)

In his turn, Chambers speculated that the problem in the modern era was not with the custom of arranged marriages – or with that of bride prices – but with the fact that money was the medium of exchange: money made women equal to anything and everything one might want to buy in a way they were not in the past. In effect, then, women so transacted became like commodities.

"We are opening up lots of things for you to think about," Thompson told Balen; things "that are confusing to us all about how to handle customs and change."

One matter, however, Thompson was sure about: certain aspects of traditional culture were needed not only by those living in rural villages, but also by those living in urban squatter settlements. Although neither she – nor anyone else present – understood fully the intricacies of Minj head payments, Thompson was convinced that such traditions provided the basis of local "cooperation." Bride prices and death compensations, for instance, were crucial to linking poorly educated Papua New Guineans with each other, whether they were living in villages or in multiethnic urban settlements (like Hanuabada, outside of Port Moresby). Without these traditions – both those distinctive to a particular group and those shared (in generalized form) among numerous groups – such people would have nothing meaningful in their lives to unite them.

Father Lak agreed that many traditional customs were good as they bound Papua New Guineans together in mutual obligations without which they would simply be "adrift." But not all customs were good. Indeed, some went against God's teachings. Children must be taught how to make Christian choices in accepting the obligations of good customs and rejecting those of bad ones. And such instruction could only be successful within Christian families, families themselves constructed from free and informed choice. The custom of head payment, Lak clearly implied – at least as it was used coercively against Miriam – was a bad custom because it could not result in such a Christian family.[3]

Although Balen, Thompson, Chambers and Lak did not – and perhaps would not – reach full agreement in their appraisal of customs such as head payment, bride price and arranged marriages, they did agree on how these should be appraised: they should not be simply accepted as inherently sacred and, hence, as fixed and binding; customs were subject to rational evaluation and modification by people such as themselves who were, as members of the middle class, "educated and modern" (to anticipate a pivotal phrase in the forthcoming court judgment). It was only from this rationalist (and, hence, ostensibly universalist) perspective that discussion of issues such as women's rights in relationship to general social order could properly take place. Correspondingly, and implicit in what was, in effect, their position of epistemological superiority, these adjudicators regarded their own lives (as distinct from those of the uneducated and traditional) as importantly the product of choice (even if, for instance, they decided to support certain traditions).

It was this perspective of the educated and modern that the court used as a reference point of the reasonable in deciding whether Miriam would be allowed to enact her choices for further education.

The judgment

Balen was successful at the preliminary hearing in convincing Justice Salamo Injia of the National Court to place Miriam in Father Lak's protective custody, pending the court's determination of whether the head payment violated constitutional and human rights, as ICRAF claimed in its application. Until that time, Miriam was not to be conveyed in head payment; furthermore, Miriam was not to be threatened either by her own kinsmen or by those demanding the compensation.

It was not until almost eight months later that Justice Injia decided the case. In his 57-page formal ruling, he stated that his evidence had derived from interviews Balen conducted.[4] After the preliminary hearing, he had instructed her to speak with "all interested leaders and any person who might have an interest in the outcome of the application, both for and against, and file affidavits" (Injia, 1997: 12).

Balen submitted five affidavits. One was from Miriam. Another was from Sam Imene, related by marriage to Miriam. Married to Miriam's father's sister, he was also Miriam's guardian and had been paying her school fees. From the Minj area, although from neither of the contending clans, Imene was a lecturer at the Highlands Agriculture College in Mount Hagen. A third affidavit was from Toni Boma, Miriam's maternal uncle on whose land Miriam's mother and sisters were living as refugees from tribal warfare. He had been warden of a correctional facility before retiring to his home village. A fourth was from John Muke, the aforementioned archeologist and member of Miriam's clan. And the last was from Balen herself.

That no other witnesses were called or consulted meant, as Judge Injia clearly recognized, that the court would base its evaluation of the custom of head payment upon the understanding of those without much immediate knowledge. Thus Judge Injia wrote: "The best evidence on 'head pay' could have come from local independent experts such as village elders, village councillors and village magistrates, but no such evidence is before me" (Injia, 1997: 14). Instead, significantly, those giving testimony were all "*educated and have been exposed to modern ways of living* and have spent much of their time away from their village" (Injia, 1997: 15; our emphasis). The judge then described himself as compelled by Muke's affidavit because "[a]lthough not a village expert in local custom, his exposition of the custom and the underlying complex social network and value impresses me" (Injia, 1997: 15). Muke's explanation was, indeed, relatively extensive and plausible and, moreover, was largely consistent with those given by Imene and Boma.

Muke's detailed description of several relevant customs was cited liberally in the ruling. He explained that in Minj culture there was a protective, nurturing relationship between a maternal clansman and his or her nephews. This relationship was recognized at the time of death, when the deceased's own clan returned his or her skull or bones, along with valuables, to the maternal kin. This return, known as the head payment, "comes under the wider nexus of life-cycle payments" (Muke, as quoted by Injia, 1997: 17). He also explained that there was a multigenerational system of marriage exchange. This was one of "prescriptive cross-cousin marriage ... [which] enables marriage-partner clans to be alternate wife-givers at [the] three (3) generational level" (Muke, as quoted by Injia, 1997: 18). Finally, Muke explained the extant "credit-debt relations" (Muke, as quoted by Injia, 1997: 19) between the groups significant to the case: as partners in warfare, they had for over 200 years exchanged five generations of women in marriage. Miriam's clan, however, was in debt to her maternal clan since women coming from the maternal clan had, over the generations, produced more offspring than those from Miriam's own clan. Moreover, Miriam's clan had for some time been living rent-free with her maternal clan.

Muke granted that in this circumstance Miriam's acceptance of marriage into her maternal clan would have been greatly welcomed, as it would have done much to restore the long-term balance between these clans. Nonetheless, he held that "Miriam's rights were not violated because she still has the same freedom as all the other Wahgi girls ... who are allowed to entertain and court any males of their own choice" (Muke, as quoted by Injia, 1997: 21). To be sure, the debt would remain an open issue until one such girl agreed to comply "with the two clans' general wish" (Muke, as quoted by Injia, 1997: 21).

Miriam, in her affidavit, stated that she was willing to be part of her father's head payment, but not willing to marry immediately and not willing to marry just anyone. She suspected, though, "that the younger generation may be too impatient" (Willingal, as quoted by Injia, 1997: 33–34), pressuring her into marriage sooner rather than later. This made her feel "lost, humiliated in the eyes of other people and ashamed at being used as a form of compensation" (Willingal, as quoted by Injia, 1997: 33) – thus echoing Chambers' concerns about commodification. Moreover, she was doing well in her education and wanted to pursue technical training, because "it is important for me to be qualified in an area where I can obtain employment as a security in life. I do not want to be a villager living on subsistence farming" (Willingal, as quoted by Injia, 1997: 33). Thus, she "went public [telling her story to the *Post-Courier*] hoping that somebody might help" (Willingal, as quoted by Injia, 1997: 34).

In judging the ICRAF application, Justice Injia took pains to understand fully the Minj custom of head payment. This he said he was enjoined to do under Section 2 of the Customs Recognition Act. Based upon the information available to him, he concluded that this Minj practice was of long standing and reflected "complex underlying social values associated with inter-tribal marriage in a complicated network of relationships" (Injia, 1997: 36). Specifically:

(1) It allows for reciprocal exchange of women between the two tribes and ensures continuity of inter-tribal relationships, tribal security and stability, etc.

(2) Because the deceased's mother married the deceased's tribe and bore them children, one of their offspring or

relatives should return to marry her mother's tribe and bear them children.

(3) Because the deceased is an offspring of one of their women and the deceased's death is attributed to the fault of his own tribesmen, it is a loss to the deceased's mother's tribe and the life lost should be replaced by another life. (Injia, 1997: 40–41)

All of this was fine, from the judge's point of view, so long as there was a "voluntary decision [on the part of] the young girl[s] of the tribe to take up the challenge when they feel like" (Injia, 1997: 39). Although there was no evidence that young girls would be necessarily forced into marriage as part of head payment, it was true that "the more closely related the girl is to the deceased and the ... [closer] the girl is to marry[ing], the more intense the pressure appears to be" (Injia, 1997: 40). Thus, Justice Injia doubted that such a decision could ever be fully voluntary and concluded that Miriam's decision was certainly not voluntary. She "did not consent to the request and felt unhappy and depressed because she was going to be included as part of her father's 'head pay'. She also felt at a loss because she did not know who her bridegroom was. She felt humiliated in the eyes of the public because she did not like the idea of being used as a form of payment" (Injia, 1997: 42).

Justice Injia stressed that the "tribesmen of Minj and their customs and customary practices, like people of any of the other small societies in Papua New Guinea, are part of modern Papua New Guinea and they are governed by our national laws. If their customs and customary practices conflict with the National Laws, they must give way to our national laws. This is a requirement of our national laws of which the Constitution reigns Supreme" (Injia, 1997: 43). Consistent with this position, he found for ICRAF on all of its arguments.

He found "that the Minj custom of asking or obliging a woman to be part of 'head pay' is an infringement of a woman's rights under Section 32" (Injia, 1997: 47) of the Constitution, guaranteeing women an equal opportunity to participate in and benefit from the development of Papua New Guinea. He found, as well, "that an open or general request for women by the deceased's mother's tribesmen as part of 'head pay' creates an obligation on all women of the deceased's tribe to find a partner from that other tribe in their lifetime and this obligation is recognized and enforced upon all young girls of that tribe. So then her first choice of marriage partner must be a man from that tribe. The more immediately related the young girl is to the deceased and the more mature she is, the more pressure is mounted. This is a direct infringement of the woman's rights under Section 32" (Injia, 1997: 48). Furthermore, Judge Injia agreed that Miriam's rights had been violated under Section 36, Freedom from Inhuman Treatment; under Section 42, Liberty of the Person; under Section 49, Right to Privacy; and under Section 52 (i), Right to Freedom of Movement. Finally, he decided that "requesting women as part of 'head pay' in the Minj area, in particular, in Miriam's case, is repugnant to the general principles of humanity – that living men or women should not be allowed to be dealt with as part of compensation payment under any circumstances" (Injia, 1997: 51). He therefore ordered that Miriam's kinsmen "abandon and desist from such custom and customary practices forthwith" (Injia, 1997: 56) and that they be "restrained from enforcing the said custom on Miriam Willingal by request, threat, force or otherwise and that Miriam Willingal be allowed to exercise her constitutional rights and freedoms without hindrance" (Injia, 1997: 57).

Justice Injia explicitly recognized that, before reaching this position, it had been necessary to take full account of the "special factors" (Injia, 1997: 51) of Papua New Guinean life. Thus, he readily granted that the

> majority of people in Papua New Guinea are uneducated and still live in villages ... [governed] by traditional customs ... from time immemorial ... [that] serve complex value systems which only they themselves best know... [Moreover, he recognized that to] one ethnic society, the custom [for example] of 'head pay' which includes women may sound offensive to women, discriminatory of women, oppressive or inhuman whereas it may not be so to the ethnic group that practices it ... [Hence], it would not be proper for any educated indigenous Papua New Guinean to pass quick judgment on the soundness or otherwise of a traditional custom of his own people or any of [the] other ethnic societ[ies] in PNG ... [Nonetheless, it seemed clear] that the framers of our constitution and modern-day legislators were thinking about a modern PNG based on ethnic societies whose welfare and advancement was based on the maintenance and promotion of good traditional customs and the discouragement and elimination of bad customs[5] as seen from the eyes of an *ordinary modern Papua New Guinean*. No matter how painful it may be to the small ethnic society concerned, such bad customs must give way to the dictates of our modern national laws. (Injia, 1997: 51–55; our emphasis)

Significantly, the guests at Thompson's lodge had taken into account these same factors before they expressed their thoughts about the case. Like Justice Injia, they had pondered the expectations and experiences of rural and urban, traditional and modern, male and female; they had decided which sort of person was appropriately to be bound by what sort of standard – whether a standard based on a local ancestral precedent or on a more universalistic vision of human rights. And, furthermore, they had thought seriously about what sorts of people were in a position to make authoritative statements, or to issue weighty opinions, about how different sorts of people in contemporary Papua New Guinea were to arrange their lives. In effect, all were concerned about the appropriate relationship between culture, class and gender in a contemporary Papua New Guinea – with the nature of social ontology in a nation composed as it was of increasingly different sorts of people. In effect, the preoccupations which animated both Justice Injia and the guests at Thompson's lodge were those of a middle class – those who, however well intentioned they regarded themselves (and however supportive in the abstract of "culture and custom as crucial symbols of identity" [Keesing, 1996: 162]), would never have submitted to a reverse process in which others defined what was best for them. It was their perspective, after all, which was being normalized into that of the ordinary modern Papua New Guinean.

On the ordinary modern Papua New Guinean

In a Papua New Guinea legal system where the constitutional guarantees of individual rights were Western-derived, this ordinary modern Papua New Guinean appeared a variant of the Western legal reference point of the "reasonable man." And, as we have just suggested, we have met at Thompson's lodge such reasonable persons: persons whose epistemological superiority allowed them to determine the complex, often puzzling questions of which local customs were good, and thus to be preserved, and which were bad, and thus to be eliminated, if Papua New Guinea were to exist as a modern nation.

Interestingly, although Justice Injia wrote with both intellectual and sympathetic understanding of how head payments functioned socially, he did not find it necessary to interview or take affidavits from anyone who actually experienced such customs as powerfully compelling. (In this regard, we note that no one providing affidavits mentioned the likely fact that the custom of head payments had cosmological significance involving, for example, substance transferences between intermarrying groups.) Even Miriam, who had been living away from her village (with Imene in Mount Hagen) so as to pursue her education, was sufficiently removed from village life both to reject a future as a subsistence farmer and to be positioned to claim the attention of the *Post-Courier.*

There was a telling consistency, thus, between Judge Injia's legal perspective (that of an ordinary modern Papua New Guinean) and the socially positioned perspective of those whose testimony he considered (that of the, mentioned earlier, "educated and ... exposed to modern ways of living" [Injia, 1997: 14–15]). Indeed, it seems fair to say that for Judge Injia (as for Balen, Thompson, Chambers and Lak) the ordinary modern Papua New Guinean *was* the educated and exposed to modern ways of living. It was this kind of person for whom, to reiterate, custom could be a matter of personal choice and decision, for whom tradition might tug, but certainly not bind. In so proceeding and adjudicating, Judge Injia was, in effect, defining only a minority of Papua New Guineans as ordinary – as reasonable – since, to cite again, the "majority of people in Papua New Guinea are uneducated and still live in villages" (Injia, 1997: 51).

Judge Injia was, hence, both delineating and validating the middle class as a distinct – at least distinctive – and elite component of Papua New Guinea's imagined national community: it was (at least primarily) the members of this class (as the educated and the modern) who had the moral and intellectual legitimacy to define the  reasonable – both for others and for themselves.

We have argued that the compo girl case was news- and courtworthy because, as a kind of morality play, it was not just a piece of a changing and problematic world; it came to embody the perspective of a particular class as to the proper arrangement of that world. In arguing that the case reflected certain distinctive interests – and interests in distinction – we have not meant to suggest that morality would have been better served if Miriam had been compelled to constitute part of the head payment. Indeed, it is hard to know what standard of reasonability other than the one applied would have better served Miriam and those like her in the culturally diverse country of contemporary Papua New Guinea: a country (as we have seen) in which "development" had been strongly promulgated as an ideal and in which education as a vital avenue to a coveted lifestyle of modern affluence had become highly restrictive.

The fulfillment of Miriam's aspirations that education would provide economic security and an escape from a life of subsistence farming, was, of course, far from assured: in Papua New Guinea's contemporary economy, unemployment was high – even among those with more educational credentials than she would likely garner.[6] But, regardless of whether her particular future would be better subsequent to the compo girl case, the futures of the uneducated and the traditional would likely be worse, inasmuch as their lives had become legitimately adjudicated by others. Correspondingly, to the degree that those of the middle class had become arbiters of good and bad customs, they became superior to those living in villages and squatter settlements; and, to the degree that these arbiters were those with education and with the (expensive) lifestyle of modernity, then their superiority had become class-based.

The essential class basis of such epistemological superiority was, it seems to us, profoundly obscured by Justice Injia's use of the word *ordinary* to describe those responsible for the "promotion of good traditional customs and the discouragement and elimination of bad customs" (Injia, 1997: 54). What this word obscured was that such "ordinary" Papua New Guineans were in the vast minority: that the ostensible baseline of reference and normalcy had become those relatively few Papua New Guineans wealthy enough to become educated and live modern lifestyles. In this way, the superiority of the "haves" could appear based primarily on knowledge and perspective rather than wealth. Correspondingly, the inferiority of the "have-nots" – those (though traditional) defined as no longer ordinary – could appear as based primarily on lack of knowledge and perspective rather than poverty.

Moreover, it seems to us that the compo girl case, because it focused on gender, was an especially good vehicle for effecting this obscuring formulation of class stratification. (Once again, we are not suggesting that morality would have been better served if Miriam had been transferred as part of a traditional head payment; nor are we suggesting that the educated and modern might not choose to follow or uphold some traditional practices.) Because Miriam's circumstance could be easily phrased in terms of universal morality, rationality and human rights, the modern could be made readily to look morally good. If, in contrast, her circumstance were viewed from a less universalist and more evidently class-based perspective, the modern would probably look more suspect.[7]

Thus, through the case of the compo girl, the revealed injuries of tradition seemed to be yielding to the hidden injuries of class: not only did those regarded as the traditional lose important authority over their lives such that they increasingly became the poor and the backward; as we shall additionally see below, people, like Miriam, who entered the urban cash economy were likely to become only marginally successful contenders for middle-class lifestyles.

Stolen moments

If the compo girl case could be viewed as a middle-class morality play about Papua New Guinean life in general, Patricia Thompson's film, *Stolen Moments: A Story of Love and Intrigue in Contemporary Mount Hagen* (1989), might be viewed as one about the proper arrangement and characteristics of middle-class life itself. We came upon this video at Thompson's lodge – the morning after our discussion about the compo girl – among a large, primarily ethnographic collection of videos about Papua New Guinean traditional life. Thompson's video, however, was different from most as it was clearly made for the middle class and it was about aspects of middle-class existence. In short, it was about how the educated and the modern fashioned their lives. To be sure, it is we who have grouped together the compo girl case and Thompson's film for discussion in this chapter, but not just because we engaged with them at the lodge. Rather, we have found both informative: both revealed the same sensibility – the same perspective – in working through aspects of concern to contemporary middle-class Papua New Guineans.

Stolen Moments focused on two middle-class Papua New Guinean couples. One couple, living in Mount Hagen, consisted of a female pharmacist and her lawyer husband; the other, living in Port Moresby, consisted of a *Post-Courier* journalist and – as he put it – his young "beautiful" but "immature" wife. The journalist traveled to Mount Hagen to cover four modernist events: a "society" variant of a traditional wedding (which turned out to be Chambers'); a pig-kill for a dead leader of national status, attended by his colleagues and many others; a Mount Hagen Chamber of Commerce and Industry meeting at which the pharmacist gave the keynote address about women's rights and capacities as equivalent to those of men; and a government reception attended by politicians from all over the country. During the course of reporting these events, the journalist fell in love with the pharmacist because she, in contrast to his wife, was a strong, intelligent woman. Meanwhile the journalist's wife back at Port Moresby was having an affair, insisting that her lover take her to nightclubs where they mingled with the smart set; the pharmacist's husband had gone away, defending at a murder trial.

Since her husband was away, the pharmacist asked her assistant to take care of her three children while she gave her keynote address. The assistant was jealous of the pharmacist. She had said "You have everything!" when she first saw her house. The pharmacist replied, "Yes we do, but we have to work very hard for it." The assistant, in the course of baby-sitting, realized that the pharmacist had not returned home for the night. Concluding that the pharmacist and the journalist were having an affair, the assistant the next morning called the journalist's wife in Port Moresby to stir up trouble by telling all. The wife became jealous – even though her lover reminded her that she was doing the same thing – and immediately went to her uncle, who was living in a squatter settlement, to get "poison." Telling him that she wanted to kill a dog or a cat, she gave him money – as a little help for his school fees.

Simultaneously, the journalist and the pharmacist, together in a rumpled hotel room, decided that their one night together would be it for them: although each found the other very attractive, she took marriage seriously and he loved his wife and was afraid of fooling around because of AIDS. But it was too late to escape without repercussions.

The journalist's wife had also telephoned the pharmacist's husband and he had returned home to confront his wife. After sending the children outside, she admitted to the affair; he broke crockery in anger (but did not hit her); she apologized, pledging that she had never before had an affair, although she had "to turn a blind eye" on his many affairs.

Back at work and having realized how her husband must have discovered her affair, the pharmacist confronted her assistant, firing her for disloyalty. In the interim, the journalist's wife had traveled to Mount Hagen and had arranged to meet the disgruntled assistant for coffee. At the coffee shop, she handed her the poison, lying about its lethal nature – saying simply that giving it to the pharmacist would prevent her from ever being desired by a man. The assistant returned to the pharmacy, apologized and was reemployed. She then solicitously offered the pharmacist coffee, into which she slipped the poison.

The pharmacist drank the doctored coffee and then left to meet her husband at an expensive hotel for lunch. There he forgave her and admitted that he too had been wrong in having affairs. Happily reconciled, they were joined at their table by some friends. However, the pharmacist, though complaining that she was not feeling well, had to return to work. She collapsed as she arrived at the pharmacy and an ambulance took her to the hospital. Feeling anxious about his wife's health, her husband went to the pharmacy and was told that she was at the hospital. The film ended without revealing whether or not the pharmacist would live or die, although prospects for her recovery looked grim. The last shots were of her small daughter sitting alone.

In what was becoming an increasingly divided Papua New Guinean polity, those of the middle class portrayed in *Stolen Moments* differed considerably from the rural villagers (and, to some extent, urban settlement dwellers) who inclined toward customs such as head payment. These latter Papua New Guineans were still likely to be significantly linked by multigenerational collective obligations – by the system of alternating credits and debts concerning life-cycle payments, prescriptive cross-cousin marriages, and military alliance or enmity. In contrast, the pharmacist and her lawyer husband (though unlikely – as we have seen – to have broken all ties with natal groups) were more likely to be significantly linked, like those of the middle class elsewhere, by noncorporate, choice-generated, relatively fluid networks based on friendships, on shared occupational and educational experiences and interests and on voluntarily assumed civic responsibilities. (And, presumably like other members of the Papua New Guinea middle class, the kinship obligations they accepted beyond their immediate nuclear – or nuclearized – families would have been more kindred than corporate-group derived.)

In its portrayal of key aspects of the social lives of affluent middle-class Papua New Guineans, the film also revealed problems in those lives. *Stolen Moments* was, after all, a tragedy. Yet, despite its ending, the film ultimately justified the perspective and sensibility, as well as the attendant lifestyle, of this middle class. Clearly educated and modern, the pharmacist and her lawyer husband generally regulated their lives according to class claims of reasonability. They recognized and accepted the importance of discipline and hard work, as shown in their educational, occupational and material attainments and in their appropriately socialized and supported children. Respecting each other's dignity and autonomy and striving to negotiate their separate and mutual interests, they worked out their differences and adjusted the course of their lives without recourse to violence and without insistence on being unconditionally in the right.

Simultaneously, however, the film implicitly recognized that some members of the middle class did not always deal with their problems in a reasonable way: for instance, men often did philander and often did move in their domestic angers from dish-breaking to wife-bashing. But the real threat to these middle-class lives appeared to come from the marginal within – from the jealous assistant and the immature wife (who had ready recourse to the dark powers of the traditional[8]). In contrast to those working out life's frictions and problems in a reasonable way, these two, as the jealous and immature, were the incompletely educated and incompletely modern.

These two could indeed be seen as troublesome within a Papua New Guinean middle-class context. To those of the middle class, they rendered problematic central aspects of their class ideology: one aspect was that middle-class privilege was the morally justifiable consequence of having met the standards of education and modernity, standards theoretically open to all. Whereas Miriam's unusual case could be readily discussed and judged so as to accord with that ideology – she must be allowed to pursue her dreams of education, etc. – the cases of the immature and the jealous were more refractory. Virtually everyone in the Papua New Guinean middle class – whether they happened to view *Stolen Moments* or not – would recognize people like the journalist's immature wife and the pharmacist's jealous assistant: the first, someone who had not worked hard for anything yet was able to demand an affluent lifestyle and social equality; the second, someone who had undoubtedly worked hard (the pharmacist's assistant had not only pursued her schooling with likely sacrifice and energy and worked regular hours as a shop assistant, but had also worked extra hours as her employer's baby-sitter) yet was unable to achieve affluence and social equality.

However, *Stolen Moments* told their stories not as evidence that a system of distinction was unfair – the unworthy were rewarded and the worthy excluded. Instead, they themselves were presented as the source of the unfairness within that system; it was they – the immature and the jealous – who, as manifestations of the unreasonable, became personally culpable for the tragic outcome of what would have otherwise been satisfying and well-led modern lives.[9]

The compo girl case was carried by the *New York Times* in part to report the court decision concerning Miriam. The article entitled, "When the Bartered Bride Opts Out of the Bargain," provided a relatively accurate account of the case in which Miriam's desire to escape her initial tribal entailments was described as motivated by her "personal ambition" to continue her education. This was a "striking sign of changing times" in a country known for its remoteness and lack of modernity (Mydans, 1997c: A4). That Miriam's personal ambition would, if she were very lucky, likely allow her a position comparable to that the pharmacist's assistant was not, of course, discussed. And, thus, was verified the triumph of a Western universal rationality (if not of capitalism).

Conclusion
On dark nights of the soul

We have shown in this book how new inequalities have come into being in a place generally characterized by its egalitarian ethos. The many stories we have told depict some of the ways the currents of global capitalism have allowed certain Papua New Guineans to use introduced forms in order both to establish new relationships and rework old ones. In short, certain Papua New Guineans have been able to redefine the ontological worth of themselves and others.

Specifically, we have shown how middle-class professionals redefined the nature of sociality; by using the connections they established through Rotary International, they (as descendants of indigenous "chiefs") claimed new privileges and affirmed new exclusions. We have shown how middle-class businesswomen redefined the causes of poverty; by using marketing schemes such as OPT, they persuaded poor women that in such schemes there was equality of opportunity when in fact there was none. We have shown how members of the grass roots, such as Godfried and Michael, were wrenched, if not infuriated, when soccer referees, golfers and politicians denied them both equality and opportunity. And we have shown, finally, how a middle-class perspective concerning law and order, human rights and constitutionality has become the standard of reasonability on which sociality itself should be based.

What we have shown, in effect, has been the manner in which currents and forms of global capitalism have featured in the transformation of commensurate differences into incommensurate differences such that those who once contended on an even footing in the same relatively fluid, political field have become regarded – redefined – as ontologically inferior.

The future course that these currents and forms might take in Papua New Guinea, particularly their long-term effect on emerging patterns of difference, was far from clear. Members of the affluent middle class themselves often recognized this upon reflection. They certainly knew that Papua New Guinea's economy was heavily dependent on forces over which they had only limited control. For example, they were aware from newspapers and television that their prosperity ultimately depended on the fluctuating value of their country's minerals, timber and agricultural products on the world market. They were also, as we have seen, not sure that Papua New Guinea would continue to be attractive for outside investment and tourism. And, in view of the sharp devaluation of the kina and the retrenchment of many civil servants, they could not even be certain that Papua New Guinea's internal market would remain viable.

Added to these economic uncertainties was the possibility of pervasive social unrest. Some of our middle-class friends talked to us about their fears. They feared attacks against property and person, of course, but they also worried about "revolution." With political corruption rampant and social services increasingly inadequate, they believed that the poor might very well become desperate. These friends surely must have been made uneasy by a newspaper article that appeared after we left the field. It reported a "total break-down in the administrative structure of the East Sepik Province . . . [with the result that] people [were] not receiving essential government services" (Fito, 1997: 1).

And many of the middle class – even those who were confident their own particular enterprises would survive – were afraid that their children might not be adequately educated to cope with an increasingly internationalized economy. They named, in this regard, several Papua New Guineans from wealthy families who had become handmaidens of Malaysian investors. They were actually business fronts, who mostly just held the briefcases of those with the real economic savvy. Moreover, the less affluent among the middle class often wondered whether they could afford to remain in town upon retirement. Or, if forced to return to their villages, they wondered what sort of life they would find there. Back in their villages, they certainly expected to be subject to powerful leveling demands and perhaps other responses prompted by accumulated envy and resentment. (In New Ireland villages, for example, many houses built of permanent materials by civil servants for use upon retirement stood empty: when the village-dwelling parents of those retiring did not wish to distinguish themselves invidiously from fellow villagers by moving into them with their children, the children felt too embarrassed to inhabit them alone [Sykes, personal communication].)

In effect, these middle-class Papua New Guineans were afraid that the commensurate differences still valued by many Papua New Guineans would be reasserted against them with renewed force. And they were afraid that the incommensurate differences inherent in world capitalism would come to marginalize virtually all, especially in a Papua New Guinea exhausted of resources. Thus, one middle class Papua New Guinean wrote to the *National* warning about the possible depletion of the country's rich supply of natural gas:

> In the interests of stimulating discussion in PNG, our people must know that there are at least three options for the use of PNG natural gas.
>
> One is sale to Queensland [where the construction of a K2.05 billion gas pipeline from Papua New Guinea to northern Queensland had been proposed by Chevron], the second, sale to southeast Asia, and the third, local utilization.
>
> Options one and two have already been talked about, but option three is yet to be widely discussed.
>
> Under that option, PNG's gas reserves must not be sold. Instead, we will keep them here and try to attract those industries that use gas to come and set up factories in PNG.
>
> We would need to provide cheap land and labour. The gas would be marketed cheaply, and electricity would be supplied by gas, reducing its cost. Then we would establish free trade zones, and give pioneer industry status to those setting up factories.
>
> With these policies in place, we could sell PNG around the world as the country that provides the cheapest energy resources. With gas reserves expected to last two to three hundred years, we would be in a position to attract hundreds of industries. They would have a competitive edge over other countries with high energy costs.
>
> With cheap energy resources, we have industrial power at our fingertips. We can flip it into the sea; or we can utilize it to turn our country into an industrialized nation within fifty years.
>
> If we export this resource, we export our opportunity, our wealth and our future. (Awi, 1997: 7)

This man – and others we knew – accurately sensed that the corollary of the unencumbered and acquisitive individuals many aspired to become was an unencumbered and acquisitive capital. To be sure, there would be some we met at venues like the Rotary and golf clubs, whose business, professional, or political skills and connections would probably prove sufficient to insure their continued access to Toyota Land Cruisers (rather than the water buffaloes Bernard Narakobi advocated), even in a resource-exhausted Papua New Guinea. But there would inevitably be others – certainly if an already stagnating economy began to shrink – who would be left behind. This would be the case even if they shared Tiger Woods' discipline, hard work and preparation. Thus, however optimistic and energetic many of the Papua New Guinean middle class might be and however important an effect they might have in driving contemporary changes in Papua New Guinea society, the future they confronted was an uncertain one of twists and turns: theirs was a world strongly affected by the shifting strategies and interests of an increasingly influential corporate and multinational capitalism. (In this regard, for instance, it will be interesting to trace the forthcoming consequences for Papua New Guinea of such phenomena as, during 1998, the dramatic fall and rise of stock prices in Asia and in the United States respectively.)

In conveying the local effects of global capitalism, we have a final tale to tell about the telling of class. Less a morality play, given its lack of the virtues and vices of already established persona, than some we have related, it certainly is a cautionary tale, given its invocation of dark nights of the soul. We conclude with it, in other words, to give all of us pause.

It was, of course, not only those in the third world such as Papua New Guineans who were worried about competitiveness in a world market: many in the United States have become equally worried about losing their competitive edge. Rosabeth Moss Kantor, a professor at Harvard Business School, explained what future middle-class viability might require: "As the global marketplace and international competition expand, as technology becomes more complex and more rapidly changing, as women and minorities seek access to the better jobs, and as growth slows (or reverses) in traditional industries" (1989: 306), many companies in order to insure survival and profits have begun to demand "flexibility" from their employees. From the perspective of employees, this has generally meant a reduction in the work force *on both worker and managerial levels*, an insistence that those employed learn to assume many different tasks (which they were often expected to finish after hours in the office or at home [see Hochschild, 1997]) and a hiring of contract laborers who work without job protection, without sick pay, without paid vacations, without medical or retirement benefits, and without hope of advancement.

Correspondingly, in a recent article in the *New York Times* which discussed these trends concerning the future of work in the United States, MIT economist, Lester Thurow bleakly warned:

> The era of lifelong company jobs with regular promotions and annual real wage increases is over. It is your responsibility to manage your own lifetime career. But you won't have a lifetime career.
>
> No one can manage his or her own career without a road map, and economic road maps cannot be drawn unless there are career ladders across companies. And they simply don't exist.
>
> In Europe, the Middle Ages saw vast numbers of masterless laborers wandering back and forth across the countryside. Walled cities and towns were the answer. The Japanese talk about the chaos of having samurai without masters. Our future is the masterless American laborer, wandering from employer to employer, unable to build a career. (1997: 9)

Importantly, the expectation that both institutions and their employees be flexible has become increasingly naturalized in the United States. Defined as characteristic of complex systems, flexibility has become a virtual imperative – a seemingly inevitable part of an evolutionary process in which only the fittest would survive (Martin, 1994). Thus, it would be very likely – since incommensurate differences have seemed to offer little ontological mercy – that when *you* lose your job, you will be assumed to be among the inflexible and nonadaptive, among the noncontenders. In this sense, you and your worth will have become fundamentally redefined by class, subject to the same processes of ontological reckoning that have been reworking the lives of Papua New Guineans.

Notes

INTRODUCTION: THE TWISTS AND TURNS OF DIFFERENCE

1 The concept of the "traditional" (or "tradition") must be understood as often invented. See, among others, Hobsbawm and Ranger, 1983. Also, the meaning of "modernity" (or "modern" or "modernist") must be understood as multifaceted and situationally contingent. Of the vast corpus of works available on modernity, we have found the following to be among the most anthropologically germane to our present study: Thompson, 1964; Burke, 1978; Berman, 1982; Harvey, 1989; Taylor, 1989; Giddens, 1991; Jameson, 1991; Sklair, 1991; Lash and Friedman, 1992; Garcia-Canclini, 1993; Miller, 1994.

2 For reviews of the literature on class as it has been used (and misused) in analyses of Pacific societies, see Hooper, n.d.; and Ogan, n.d.a and n.d.b. See, as well, Turner, 1984; Wolfers, 1992; Howard and Rensel, 1994.

3 Papua New Guinea has, since 1975, been an independent country composed of the eastern half of the second largest island in the world. (The western half, known as Iryan Jaya, has become part of Indonesia.) At the turn of the nineteenth century, the northern part of today's Papua New Guinea was colonized by the Germans, and the southern part by the British. Prior to World War One, British New Guinea became a Territory of Australia, called Papua. Shortly after World War One, German New Guinea became the Mandated Territory of New Guinea. Although under the formal jurisdiction of the League of Nations, it too was under Australian supervision. Both portions came under a unified Australian administration subsequent to World War Two. Throughout the period of Australian control, Papua and New Guinea were treated largely as colonies.

4 Our claim that *many* Papua New Guinean societies were indigenously characterized by a strenuous egalitarianism (at least among men) would not, of course, be contradicted by the fact that in "some [cases] there were definite systems of rank and chiefdomship"

(Strathern, 1982: 47). Such a system of chiefly precedence appears to have once existed, for example, in Manus (Carrier and Carrier, 1989). (This was, though, undermined in its economic basis – and, hence, efficacy – early in the colonial era.) A somewhat comparable instance of hierarchy was incipient among the Sepik River Manambu, predicated on control of ritual knowledge acquired through exchange relations (Harrison, 1985). (However, in our view, this hierarchy was likely to remain incipient in part because intergroup exchange relationships shifted frequently in response to political and military exigencies.)

Such cases aside, it is important to note that, where substantial (though lesser) indigenous inequalities did exist, the likelihood of their fixed and lasting instantiation was often mitigated by key structures and processes. Thus, for instance, while Hagen big men of the Papua New Guinea Highlands monopolized the circulation of valuable shells and relied importantly on the labor of their multiple wives and junior kinsmen, they were not assured of the "direct reproduction of their status within their own families ... The possibility of switching group affiliation is explicitly recognised, and it is a built-in feature of flexibility. Pigs, a major wealth item, can be reared quickly, and they breed in multiple fashion. Crops are not stored and, in Hagen, there is little emphasis on garden magic or other forms of knowledge exclusive to elders as such" (Strathern, 1982: 47).

Comparably, in appraising the *possibility* of relatively permanent relationships of inequality in those Highland regions of intensive production (areas where such inequalities might be most expected), Modjeska concluded that these relationships were in practice unlikely: "[S]o long as production can be contained within kinship-structured units, there is ... no conflict of interests [generating and marking levels of inequality between men] that an inventive adjustment of social practices consistent with the tribal ethos of exchange, sacrifice and equality cannot contain" (1982: 108).

We must, however, recognize that many of those cultures often described as egalitarian may not have extended equality to women (see Jolly and Mosko, 1994). Interestingly, this gender-based inequality may have sometimes sustained male equality. Thus, Modjeska suggested that "inequality among men must be contained at some level and cannot be expanded without limit, lest breakdowns in male solidarity should threaten the lineage's security *vis-à-vis* other lineages and undermine as well the collective exploitation of women" – on whose productive activities men were dependent (1982: 108). Indeed, Modjeska concluded that Duna men exploited women in a class-like manner within the indigenous economic system – a position he reiterated in later publications (where he, however, changed his view about how best to diagnose exploitation, shifting his focus from processes of production to those of exchange [see Modjeska, 1995]).

5 To be sure, money could provide the basis of difference of degree rather than of kind such that individuals might be placed on a continuum according to the amount of money possessed. Indeed, within systems of commensurate differences, money could figure (along with pigs, shells, wives, ritual knowledge, trading partners and allies) as a determinant of power. (For Melanesian examples see Gewertz and Errington, 1995; Foster, 1998; and the collection of essays in Akin and Robbins, eds., 1999.) However, within systems of incommensurate differences as those of class, money was likely to provide the basis for differences of kind because it provided differential access to modes of making more money. Moreover, within class systems, power did not ordinarily rest on the creation of personal followings of the nonaffluent through the redistribution of wealth items like money. In other words, within class systems, the rich generally got richer and primarily associated with one another. Bourdieu aptly characterizes central elements of this contrast between systems: "it is not by lavishing generosity, kindness, or politeness, on his charwomen (or on any other 'socially inferior' agent), but by choosing the best investment for his money, or the best school for his son, that the possessor of economic or cultural capital perpetuates the relationship of domination which objectively links him with his charwoman and even her descendants" (1977: 189–90).

6 Certainly, class systems have (in varied degree) allowed some mobility. Thus, instances might be cited in which, for example, an exceptionally talented laborer's son won a scholarship to a private school and, having done well, rose in class position. Indeed, such stories of the heroic overcoming of adversity have been often promoted as part of an ideology defining class differences as products of volition and hard work rather than of birth and privilege. (See chapter 2 below, in particular, for a Papua New Guinea example of such an ideology in practice; see, as well, Errington and Gewertz, 1988.)

7 This problem has again become critical during 1998 as this book goes to press. The exchange value of the kina has recently dropped dramatically in part because of "El Nino" (such that, for instance, an acute and prolonged drought has reduced not only cash-cropping but hydraulically dependent gold mining) and of weakened Asian economies (such that, for instance, Malaysian timbering operations in Papua New Guinea were no longer economically feasible).

8 This cutback in governmental funding has placed tremendous pressure on, for instance, church-run schools and medical facilities. As governmental spending for services declined, these church operations not only had to cope with a decreasing amount of governmental subsidy,

but with an increasing number of clients spilling over from ever more inadequate government facilities.

9 Turner has stated that Papua New Guinea has been the fourth largest investor in Queensland real estate (1990: 72).

10 It has been important to us in several previous publications to demonstrate that the role of Papua New Guinea as the diametrical "other" in the Western imagination – as the "primitive," as the "last unknown" – is an empirically inaccurate and politically inappropriate one. See in this regard, Gewertz and Errington, 1991b and 1997; Errington and Gewertz, 1995.

11 On elites, see Bottomore, 1964; Marcus, 1983.

12 One example of this perspective was related by Father Cherobim Dambui (whom we discuss in chapter 5 below) – the acting bishop of Wewak and a former provincial premier. He said that whenever he thought about the contemporary political scene, he recalled an event occurring in 1969, just after he had finished high school. In a relatively remote part of the Sepik, he met a man who had "just come out of the Stone Age." The man was curious about Dambui's outboard motor, for he had never seen one before. He listened to the motor and thought it was "the heartbeat of a living thing. The motor made no sense to him." Meeting this man caused Dambui to think about his grandmother (from the Sepik River village of Timbunke). When she was twelve, she saw the first white men come up the river in a steam-powered ship. Her understanding of the white man must have been much like the understanding of the man seeing Dambui's outboard for the first time: it was "miles away" from Dambui's own understanding of the world. No wonder, he thought "the country is confused," for "we're like actors who have been brought on a stage and are not sure who is supposed to play what role. The people of the country are at different stages of seeing the common picture: some still see it from the Stone Age; others see it from the moon and beyond."

13 The three large Chambri home villages of Indingai, Kilimbit and Wombun were located south of the Sepik River on an island-mountain within Chambri Lake. Chambri spoke a non-Austronesian language of the Nor Pondo family, subsisted on fish which they bartered for sago produced by non-Chambri, and embraced an elaborate ritual system predicated on patriclan-based totemic prerogatives. (See Gewertz, 1983, and Errington and Gewertz, 1987 for a discussion of their "indigenous" social and ritual organization.)

From the 1930s through the 1950s, Chambri began to leave their home villages in increasing numbers, many for Wewak. At first Wewak was a point of departure for Chambri labor migrants on their way to the plantations of New Britain and New Ireland; or it was a place of religious training for the Catholic mission catechists before they were stationed throughout the Sepik. However, by the early 1960s, Chambri began to travel to Wewak for other purposes and for longer periods of time: they came to supervise their children who, having completed the limited schooling available at Chambri, were attending mission schools in Wewak; or they came to watch out for their kin who were receiving treatment at the Wewak hospital. In order to provide housing for themselves they eventually rented from indigenous landowners a small area adjacent to one of the main roads. Here they built the makeshift houses that formed the nucleus of what became the Chambri Camp.

By the early 1970s Chambri began to travel to Wewak in ever-increasing numbers, usually staying with those kin or covillagers already living in Chambri Camp. They came primarily to earn money to take or send home. But they also came to see what town life was like. Women who came to sell fish might stay several months before returning to Chambri; the men who accompanied them or those who came alone might look for jobs and stay longer. They built houses or additions to existing structures for themselves from whatever was available – bush materials, scavenged pieces of sheet metal and even cardboard – and squeezed these in as they could.

And, although few had intended to stay very long and none had long-term claim on the land, the camp came to look and function like a Chambri village, with plantings of fruit and coconut trees under which chickens, ducks, and the occasional pig foraged. Chambri Camp became increasingly crowded, but was never a slum: outhouses were built on the periphery; separate bathing places for men and women were cleared along the banks of a nearby stream; yards were swept and trash burned. Men met in the three modest but functional men's houses which, significantly, were named after the first men's houses in each of the three Chambri villages. Eventually, many of those living in the camp considered it their home and did not plan to return to Chambri at all, except perhaps for brief visits. In their urban history and lives, Chambri were, we think, like many Sepik River peoples who had come to inhabit the dozens of squatter communities throughout Wewak.

14 It is the case as Thomas, 1991; O'Hanlon, 1993; Miller, 1994; and Foster, 1997 (among others) made clear, that different peoples have, to some extent, reconfigured the globally traversing products of capitalist production in culturally distinctive ways: Pepsi in Papua New Guinea may not necessarily have meant the same thing or have been used in the same way as Pepsi in the United States.

15 Concerning the perpetuation of ethnic allegiances that cross-cut class lines, we might mention that the (thus far) successful objections to World Bank attempts to privatize land were importantly generated by

university students returning to their home areas to alert coethnics of the threat to their mutual interests in continuing collective patterns of land ownership.

16 Reliable population figures have been hard to come by and evaluate in Papua New Guinea. For instance, many urban dwellers not only resided in difficult-to-census squatter settlements, but often practiced circular migration to home villages and other parts of Papua New Guinea. In addition, demography has become highly politicized (see, for example, Cole, 1993; Hayes, 1994 and 1995; Fry, 1997). There were controversies over the rate of urban growth and over if that rate suggested a trajectory of development or of chaos. There were corresponding debates about whether funds should be spent to address urban problems or to make rural life more attractive. And, of course, there were electoral disputes about who should vote where. The urban population figure we used of 20 percent seemed conservative generally and, in fact, was definitely low for the Chambri and probably low for the East Sepik Province as a whole. (In fact, in earlier publications [Errington and Gewertz, 1997; Gewertz and Errington, 1998] we used a figure of 25 percent, which might well be more accurate.) In any case, it had become evident that a very substantial and increasing proportion of Papua New Guineans have been spending considerable time in towns. Moreover, even those who remained village-based, have become significantly affected by urban life and expectations. We wish especially to thank John Ballard, Dan Jorgensen, William Standish, and Karen Sykes for providing information and insight about such demographic issues.

17 There has been anthropological debate concerning whether "traditional" societies were amenable to class analysis. After all, in many of these societies, men often compelled the labor of women; elders, that of juniors. (As this debate has figured in the anthropology of Papua New Guinea, see, in particular, Godelier, 1977; Modjeska, 1982 and 1995; Strathern, 1982 and 1984; Josephides, 1985.) Our own position is similar to that of Keesing (1976): he argued that, strictly speaking, class societies were ones in which classes constituted an overall system of economically based privileges and discriminations (such that each class was defined relative to the others); that they were ones in which class membership was both somewhat open (such that sex could not be a primary qualification) yet substantially closed (such that relative age could not be a primary qualification). However, like Keesing, we agree that class-like analysis could be productively applied to many societies because it "leads one to seek out the economic bases of political power, to see the uses to which this power is put by those who have it, to see internal conflict between those in a society who have opposing interests as a driving force for change,

and to see 'a society' as a temporary stage in the unfolding of social process" (1976: 344).

Yet, whether one thinks it appropriate to apply either a class-based or class-like analysis to both "traditional" and "modern" Papua New Guinea society, our distinction between commensurate or incommensurate differences would still hold. This is so, we argue, because the "class" relations in each case were differently constituted, reproduced and sustained. (In this regard, see Strathern [1985; 1988] for a broad depiction of the differences between Melanesian and Western regimes of value.)

18 See, also, Runciman, 1969; Giddens, 1973; Curtain, 1984; Lipset, 1985; Burris, 1986 and 1987; Schama, 1987; Wiley, 1987; Ortner, 1991; Wacquant, 1991; Ogan and Wesley-Smith, 1992; Hooper, n.d.; Ogan, n.d.a. and n.d.b.

19 That the Papua New Guinea affluent generally distinguished themselves from the grass roots with respect to lifestyles did not preclude them from sharing, as Weber (1968) stressed, a range of often situational interests. Some of these common, or at least overlapping, interests have already been suggested in our earlier examples about lack of polarization. Others will be presented later as in a discussion of shared law-and-order concerns.

20 According to Papua New Guinea's *Quarterly Economic Bulletin*, "there was a decrease of 3.3 percent in [those actually working in] the labour force in 1996" (Yombon, 1997). Moreover, as Dr. Ila Temu, the director of Papua New Guinea's Mineral and Resources Development Corporation, was quoted as saying, "the PNG economy has grown over the last 20 years by an average annual rate of less than one percent, compared to an annual population growth of 2.3 per cent ... [making it] a poor country [in which] something has obviously gone very wrong as all the wealth that has been generated is not having any impact on the lives of the people" (Kuble, 1997).

21 In Errington and Gewertz, 1988, we argued that the idea of the exemplar is likely to be important primarily when the path to eminence is either obscured or highly restricted. Such was increasingly the case, as was the increasing importance of exemplars, in Papua New Guinea.

22 As we elaborate in chapter 2 below, most squatters received only sporadic and limited income from the sale of such artifacts as carvings and baskets to tourists or from the sale of such items as beer on the black market.

23 In the following pages, we have sought to protect the identities of those about whom we have written. The only actual names we have used have been of public figures, including national politicians, and of some of our Chambri friends in accord with their wishes.

24 See, also, Thompson, 1978; McKendrick, Brewer and Plumb, 1985; Earle, 1989; Carrier, 1995; Hunt, 1996.

1 THE MIDDLE CLASS – THE (NEW) MELANESIAN WAY

1 An excellent analysis of the changing social roles of the Rotary Club and other service organizations is Charles, 1993. We have also found significant data about Rotary in: University of Chicago Social Science Survey Committee, 1934; Marden, 1935; Nicholl, 1984.

2 Clubs, of course, had long been organized to provide mutual business support for members of the middle class. See, for instance, Jacob, 1981; Brewer, 1985.

3 Rotary Clubs, to be sure, were shaped by their varying sociocultural contexts. Thus, according to Charles, 1993, European Rotary Clubs were considerably more formal than American Rotary Clubs.

4 Rydell, 1984, and Bradford and Blume, 1992, both demonstrated the remarkable resonance America's turn-of-the century world's fairs had for the millions who visited them.

5 As we mentioned in our introduction, according to local usage, Europeans, Filipinos and Chinese were all categorized as "expats." However, when socially significant, they would be referred to by place of origin, as we do here. We might also reiterate that the term *national* was used interchangeably with *Papua New Guinean*. We, as others, were likely to use the latter when the former might be ambiguous, as in a *national leader*.

6 Since returning home, we received a letter from our grass-roots research assistant during our 1996 field trip. He wryly described what had happened to the money we had given him upon our departure. It had all been distributed to kin, who made compelling claims upon him which he simply could not refuse.

7 As we suggested in the note 4 of the introduction, the colonial intrusion might have actually flattened hierarchy by undermining the economic bases of chiefly precedent (see Carrier and Carrier, 1989). Yet, we should point out that the distinctions within Papua New Guinean societies early in the contact period, whether of flattened hierarchy or not, might have become restratified as class differences by the same colonial (and postcolonial) processes.

8 Although there has been much debate of late concerning the ontological status of those described in the literature on Pacific societies as "big men" and "chiefs" (see Ryan, 1978, and the collection of articles in Jolly and Mosko, 1994), we are interested here only in a contemporary rhetorical use of these terms.

9 In fact, if the cultural bases allow (and perhaps even if they do not), chiefly claims by the most elite may be followed by formal chiefly

installation. We were not, therefore, surprised to learn that several national politicians holding especially desirable senior posts – posts which conveyed numerous opportunities, both licit and illicit – were given chiefly titles by their kin and constituents. Not only have such men of long-term eminence as Sir Michael Somare, often described as the father of the country, been transformed into "the chief" (by which title he is generally known throughout the Sepik and beyond), so also have others of more recent prominence. Thus, during our period of research, both of Papua New Guinea's daily newspapers carried front-page pictures of a chiefly installation. Each newspaper published captions such as "Paramount chief is a new title for Deputy Prime Minister Chris Haiveta, pictured above shaking hands with leaders at Iokea village after being 'crowned'" (Tannos, 1996: 1).

10 As we shall see more clearly in the next chapter, middle-class charity functioned to differentate those who could give from those who must receive: while the egalitarian redistribution of many indigenous Papua New Guinean exchange systems mantained socioeconomic commensurability, charity constructed and structured difference.

11 The Rotary Club acted, in other words, much as an etiquette book. As Schlesinger, 1946 pointed out, etiquette books become important precisely when people are trying to move up in the world.

12 On 28 April 1996 a gunman killed thirty-five tourists visiting the site of an old penal settlement at Port Arthur, Tasmania.

13 Members of the Papua New Guinean middle class frequently referred to – sometimes bragged about – their cosmopolitan experiences as marked by travels abroad. Indeed, their curricula vitae would enumerate such trips.

14 Yet, expat Rotary members sometimes feared that, though welcome to visit, they might find it difficult to join the club of their choice if they returned home – given how "snobby" clubs were supposed to be, for example, in Sydney.

15 As Carrier, 1995 has made clear, the disjunctions between gifts and commodities frequently blur in people's activities – whether in Melanesia or in the United States. Yet, as he also has made clear, these disjunctions were rhetorically and, hence, sociologically compelling. What the Rotary dinner-auction accomplished was more than the merging which goes on in everyday life. Rather, it was a merging of the rhetorical salience of the categories themselves.

16 We did hear, for instance, economically influential businesspeople say they were going to make things difficult for companies which could easily have contributed to the auction but did not do so.

17 For literature about the social context of auctions see Errington, 1987, and Smith, 1990.

18 Carrier has described a somewhat comparable change in eighteenth-

century England with the development "of the free, independent individual [for whom gifts are important but] who is neither bound to give nor bound by giving" (1995: 157). In this regard, we would not deny that some nationals might have viewed aspects of the competitive donating and bidding as analogous to more traditional competitive giving of, for example, pigs or pearl shells. However, these nationals must also have been aware that the Rotary auction was in ambiance and structure significantly different from traditional exchanges: while often exuberant, such prestations were rarely jovial; while competitive, they were rarely characterized by immediate, face-to-face escalations; while led by prominent individuals they were fundamentally engagements between collectivities. Conversely, most expats would readily recognize the Rotary auction as directly analogous to charity fundraisers common in places like Australia and America.

19 During the Depression, the University of Chicago's Social Science Survey analyzed Chicago's first (the original) Rotary Club (1935) and reported what it considered to be a failing: Rotarians emphasized "service" but rarely considered serious social and political problems or injustices. This was still the case in 1996 – at least in Wewak – where Rotarians stressed the amelioration of a basically fair system rather than the change of a basically unjust one.

20 Public joking and jibing were featured in all of the large-scale social events we attended with members of the middle class – all of which involved masters of ceremonies, auctioneers, bookies, or other purveyors of dangerous humor.

21 Nationals were teased less than expats at all public events, even when the master of ceremonies was a national. This was the case, we think, for the same reasons Apaches were usually careful not to go too far in their humorous jokes about the whiteman (see Basso, 1979): when humor became too real, it spilled from its play frame and provoked a socially disruptive response.

2 HOW THE GRASS ROOTS BECAME THE POOR

1 All of Papua New Guinea's four major newspapers (the English-language *Post-Courier*, *National*, and *Independent* and the Neo-Melanesian *Wantok*) would frequently publish letters to the editor with titles such as "Blame the Crime on Wide Rich–Poor Gap" (Mai, 1996), or editorials with titles such as "Families Caught in a Vicious Wage Trap" (*National*, 1996a) also expressing this anger.

Here is an example of a typical text:

WHY does the law and order problem increase despite the government's declaration of 1996 as law enforcement year?

Asking the WHY question and using a bit of reflection would . . . [cause one to] realize the root cause of the law and order problem . . . as the cancerous sickness eating away at the fabric of our society.

The [poor] people use criminal elements as a means to attain an end. That is, the people kill, rob, etc. to signify their frustration over the government's management of the country's affairs to meet their basic needs and services like food, shelter, water supply, health services, education, roads, electricity, employment, which are not provided by the government or if provided, not made accessible to all the people out of ignorance or imposition of high fees on the services which are supposed to be free. (Taka, 1996: 10)

2 These obligations ranged from mundane assistance with, for example, subsistence costs and school fees, to ritual contributions to, for example, bride prices and death ceremonies.

3 For informative analyses of comparable instantiations of modernist claims concerning middle-class expectations, see McKendrick, Brewer and Plumb, 1985; Earle, 1989; Carrier, 1995; Hunt, 1996.

4 SWIT's initiative had originally begun as a project of the East Sepik Council of Women (ESCOW), one of the more durable and successful women's development organizations in Papua New Guinea. Significantly, there had been a falling out among those who eventually led SWIT and other members of ESCOW concerning, among other things, whether ESCOW should remain, in large measure, rural-focused. SWIT's leaders thought not: they all were supporters of a former and eventually deposed ESCOW president who had wanted a more urban engagement, one that would draw national, even international, attention and assistance.

5 In rural and urban contexts, but especially in urban ones, religious affiliation was increasingly described and experienced as a matter of choice, as any reader of Weber, 1956, would have predicted. Thus, although the majority of Chambri remained true to what they considered their Catholic "mother" church, each year more were joining other congregations. For an analysis of the rhetorics of religious choice as they came to form and transform Papua New Guinea allegiances and commitments, see Errington and Gewertz, 1995.

6 This handout mentality would, from the perspective of SWIT's leadership, be well illustrated in Taka's letter to the editor, cited in note 1 above. This letter blames the law and order problem on lack of government services.

7 We were concerned that OPT was a pyramid scheme, more interested in raising money through membership fees than in providing a service. Our inquiries about OPT's reputability to the Australian High Commission in Port Moresby were unanswered. However, in response to questions we later put to the director, we were phoned and faxed by OPT representatives from their Australian office. We eventually con-

cluded that OPT probably would provide some service to some Papua New Guineans, but doubt that most would receive value for their membership fees.

8 Some of our more prosperous Chambri friends shared this image of a life merging the traditional with the modern. Thus they fantasized about retiring to their home villages where, with advanced telecommunications, they could remain comfortable and connected. Indeed, the state-run telephone company advertised its services with posters depicting such villages fairly sprouting with antennas, solar panels and satellite dishes. On the other hand, many of the elite to whom we spoke said they would prefer to visit rather than live permanently in villages, no matter what amenities they might find there.

9 There were some international markets for Papua New Guinea handicrafts, but not, we think, for the quantities and prices producers were imagining. Moreover, though various nongovernment organizations including the World Wildlife Fund purchased small numbers of net bags – recognizing that a market existed for the natural products of remote rain-forest dwellers – such schemes were not directed at urban producers.

10 Educated Papua New Guineans, such as SWIT's leaders, often derided the grass roots for tendencies to cargoism. This does not, of course, preclude the possibility that indigenous cargoistic expectations may have, in fact, swayed both SWIT leaders and followers. Such a possibility might seem supported by the propensity of many of the Papua New Guinean elite – as well as many of the grass roots – to subscribe readily to get-rich-quick schemes, such as OPT, that would dramatically transform their circumstances. Yet, this propensity does not demonstrate necessary continuity with indigenous Melanesian cargoism since many Australians, for instance, also were convinced by OPT's (and comparable) rhetoric. (Alternatively, if Lindstrom, 1993 was correct that cargoistic desires primarily reflected, not indigenous Melanesian epistemologies, but Western commodity lust, then perhaps all within OPT's global reach might be regarded as cargoists.)

3 THE REALIZATION OF CLASS EXCLUSIONS

1 And, it should be added, Woods deserved much of his heroic status for having broken the color barrier in a very white exclusionary sport; in fact, even subsequent to his success, he has had to contend with racist remarks from his fellow golfers.

2 Much could be said from varying perspectives about such a complex game as golf. Indeed, many have been stimulated by the aesthetics of the game and its setting into lyrical description. For two recent, compelling examples see Updike, 1996, and Klein, 1997.

3 Other media-promoted occasions in Papua New Guinea for defining nuclear families through acts of periodic consumption were Father's Day, Valentine's Day, Christmas and back-to-school sales. Not all members of the middle class, of course, equally embraced these occasions, although many did feel compelled to accede to at least some of their strictures. Thus, one man wrote a letter to the *National* complaining:

> I am wondering if there can be some sort of regulation put in place covering the inherited foreign customs currently evident in this nation of ours.
>
> Each year there are special days such as Mother's Day, Father's Day, Valentine's Day, birthdays and children's days, and so on.
>
> We can reasonably keep some of these days, in line with our moral values – but Father's Day and Mother's Day? What on earth is PNG up to?
>
> I come from a society where helping out in the garden or clearing bush will always make the father and mother remember their sons and daughters. Mother's Day and Father's Day is an everyday gift.
>
> These "days" mean that the average family budget is in excess of K50 per occasion to make sure of the day's success; this is forced on the family's net income. . . .
>
> For the record on Sunday, Sept. 7, I was forced to buy something for myself in excess of K30. I had not catered for that expense, but was forced into it because it was one of those externally inherited days.
>
> Please PNG can we think about the way we adopt these "days" and appreciate our own moral values?
>
> Why not a Tumbuna [ancestor] Day? (Marcus, 1997: 7)

4 We do not mean to suggest that village- or settlement-dwelling Chambri, for example, felt no affection for their mothers (either biological or classificatory). However, they did not seem to experience, and certainly did not express, a greatly elaborated subjectivity, much less a sense that the nuclear family was the primary source and site of such a subjectivity.

5 Such international games could, of course, take on local configurations. Perhaps the most dramatic example of this was the case of "Trobriand Cricket" (see Kildea and Leach, 1975).

6 At that time, Somare was Wanjik's political superior in a number of respects. He was the leader of their Pangu Party. Moreover, he not only held the at-large seat for the entire East Sepik Province, but, in so doing, was governor of the province. Wanjik held only one of the numerous local seats.

7 It was likely that Wanjik did lie to many of his potential constituents concerning what he would do for them. Yet, as we suggested in Errington and Gewertz, 1995: 135–55, it would have been very difficult for any Papua New Guinean politician to win election without making many unfulfillable promises. As it turned out, Wanjik was among the

nearly 50 percent of those seeking reelection who were not returned to parliament.

8 For example, Nike has been widely criticized of late for paying huge sums to secure the endorsement of sports' celebrities – including Tiger Woods – while paying its third world manufacturing workers in Vietnam and elsewhere virtually nothing.

4 THE HIDDEN INJURIES OF CLASS

1 Such examples of first- – or early – contact experiences in which locals appeared transfixed (and the purveyors, perhaps, virtually godlike) by unfamiliar manufactured commodities could be multiplied (see Thomas, 1991 for an interesting analysis of what was actually transacted). In an oft-cited photograph, for example, a Papua New Guinea girl was portrayed wearing a number of used flash bulbs as a necklace (Clifford, 1988; Torgovnik, 1990; Gewertz and Errington, 1991b). Likewise, the Dutch acquisition of Manhattan from its Native American residents was depicted in many schoolbooks as facilitated by the keen local interest in novel trade goods. Comparably, Hawaiians were described as so eager for iron that Captain Cook and his men could acquire a pig for a nail or two (Obeyesekere, 1992). (Concerning comparative commercial apotheoses, we might note that one of the Leahy brothers, Dan, became knighted for his contributions to Papua New Guinea's commercial life. He, thus, fared rather better in the long term for his efforts to open up the world for trade than did Captain Cook. Cook may have been in the right place with the right "product," but was certainly there one time too many.)

2 Concerning the social life of things under global capitalism, see, among others: Appadurai, 1986; Thomas, 1991; Tobin, 1992; Kearney, 1995; Miller, 1995; Gewertz and Errington, 1996.

3 We must recognize that, with respect to (exogenously derived) novel objects, local cultures may have had only a relatively brief period in which they could define them exclusively within their own scheme of existing values. Thus, the period Thomas described in *Entangled Objects* wherein that which was "given does not tell us what was received" (1991: 108) was likely to have been only a relatively brief one.

4 More accurately, as we later discovered, the whistle Godfried desired was only one of a number of models marketed under the brand name "Fox 40."

5 The reasons why a particular group might be selected and funded to go to a cultural show were complex. These often concerned efforts by politicians to gain the support of cultural groups as voting blocks by providing patronage to influential local leaders. See Errington and Gewertz, 1996, for a discussion of an instance of such patronage at work.

5 THE PROBLEM(S) OF THE POOR

1 There had been, for example, Trevor Kennedy's much publicized speech in Port Moresby on 8 May 1996. Kennedy, chairman of the Australian-based company Oil Search, which had large investments in Papua New Guinea, was reported as saying that there was "an escalating level of nervousness" among international investors because of the "uncertainty" created by Papua New Guinea's "appalling law and order situation" coupled with a "current lack of focus and discipline in the government ... and the failing infrastructure" (as quoted by Miria, 1996: 1). The speech drew immediate fire from Prime Minister Chan, who called for Kennedy's resignation. However, to judge by letters to the newspapers as well as by conversations with our middle-class friends, many thought Kennedy – though perhaps blunt – was speaking the simple truth.

2 The petition, which Deborah was asked to write, stated:

> We the people of Wewak Town – whether we be settlement, or compound or upper-covenant dwellers – whether we be grass roots, or laborers, or mission workers, or professionals – we are *all tired of living in fear.* We have come together in signing this petition to take a first step toward gaining control over our lives. We wish our fellow citizens and our duly elected government officials to know that we will insist on finding a solution to the law and order problems which plague our lives. By signing this petition we indicate our unity as citizens who have the right to a peaceful existence. Also, in signing this petition we indicate our willingness as members of a united community to work together to insure this right. We will submit this petition to the Governor of the Province, to other relevant officials, and to the press to inform them – to repeat – that WE ARE TIRED OF LIVING IN FEAR.

3 The lyrics included these lines (in translation from the Neo-Melanesian): "My father hits my mother and I have become an angry child. / I want to burn down my house. / I want to run away and stay with relatives. / Father, the law forbids you to hit your wife, to spend money on beer without thinking about food. / All your children will turn out badly."

4 In this regard, we were reminded of American news programs (such as the *NewsHour,* with Jim Lehrer) where the display of various – but mostly mainstream – perspectives on a controversial issue provided something for everyone, except serious news analysis.

5 This is consistent with Bateson's discussion of the social dynamics generating situational conformity to a particular ethos (1958: 119–22).

6 The rehabilitation coordinator later told us that much of his analysis of Papua New Guinea's crime problems came from *Law and Order* (Hopkins and McPhedren, 1985). He had obtained this book while accompanying a Papua New Guinea politician as police bodyguard

during a conference in England on politics and law. Looking at his copy, we could see such topic headings as "Who are the victims?" and "Whose law, whose order?"

7 One of our expat friends was sure that much of the crime committed in her middle-class neighborhood was done by those she called "the bats" – the alienated and spoiled children of high-ranking civil servants who hung out together at night.

6 CLASS AND THE DEFINITION OF REASONABILITY

1 This statistic was taken from Foster, 1997, who was quoting Robie, 1995.

2 The *New York Times* had been running feature articles about Papua New Guinea, all dealing with aspects of social change. Thus, in addition to the story of the compo girl, there was one about the problems of uniting numerous tribal groups into a nation (Mydans, 1977a); another, about the proliferation of youth gangs in urban centers (Mydans, 1997b); another, about the dauntingly complex missionary project of translating the Bible into the many diverse languages of the country and of (fully) converting the people (Mydans, 1997d); and another, about street crime throughout the country (Mydans, 1997e). This interest in Papua New Guinea (unusual for any major United States newspaper) followed worldwide concern that its prime minister would face army insurrection for hiring mercenaries to control rebels on the island of Bougainville. Western perceptions of contemporary Papua New Guinea sociopolitical life were in this way being shaped by stories of the wrenching birth pangs of modernity.

3 We had often heard expressions by Catholic and Protestant leaders elsewhere in Papua New Guinea of similar sentiments concerning the importance of appropriate socialization in nuclear families, and suspect it had become ubiquitous Christian rhetoric. See, in this regard, not only chapter 5, but Errington and Gewertz, 1995, and Gewertz and Errington, 1996.

4 We wish to thank Judge Warwick Andrew of the Papua New Guinea Supreme Court for having provided us with a transcript of Judge Injia's formal ruling on the compo girl case.

5 Although Justice Injia granted that the "meaning of the term 'General Principles of Humanity' has never been judicially considered by the courts" (Injia, 1997: 50), he claimed that its "ordinary meaning has never been doubted" (Injia, 1997: 50). To support this claim, he cited three Papua New Guinea cases in which certain customs were judged repugnant to these general principles: customs of cannibalism, of payback killing and of mutilating adulterers.

6 Miriam was evidently taking correspondence courses – which cost

K80 each – through the College of Distance Education (CODE), presumably to improve the grades she had received on her Grade 10 examinations. These grades had likely been inadequate to gain her admission to any of the Papua New Guinea professional training colleges, much less to either of the country's universities. If she did manage to improve her grades and gain entry, she would undoubtedly have to "self-sponsor" at considerable personal cost. Clearly she had not been an outstanding student and probably would not receive sufficient credentials to gain a very good job.

7 Western missionaries and unilinear evolutionists often spoke about gender relations involving the proper care of, and respect for, women as diagnostic of "civilization" (Thomas, 1994).

8 Middle-class Papua New Guineans usually had retained considerable respect for traditional powers pertaining to sorcery and poison.

9 As we have seen in chapter 5, there were other threats to a well-lived middle-class life, such as assault and robbery.

References

Akin, David and Joel Robbins, eds., 1999 *Money and Modernity: State and Local Currencies in Melanesia*. Pittsburgh: University of Pittsburgh Press.

Amarshi, Azeem, Kenneth Good and Rex Mortimer, 1979 *Development and Dependency: The Political Economy of Papua New Guinea*. Oxford: Oxford University Press.

Anderson, Benedict, 1983 *Imagined Communities*. London: Verso.

Appadurai, Arjun, ed., 1986 *The Social Life of Things: Commodities in Cultural Perspective*. Cambridge: Cambridge University Press.

AusAid, 1995 *Papua New Guinea: Improving the Investment Climate*, International Development Issue, 39. National Capital Printing, Canberra.

Awi, Aitabe, 1997 "Use PNG Gas Locally to Develop Industrial Power." *National*, 3 September, p. 7.

Basso, Keith, 1979 *Portraits of the Whiteman*. Cambridge: Cambridge University Press.

Bateson, Gregory, 1958 *Naven*. Stanford: Stanford University Press.

Battaglia, Debbora, 1995 "On Practical Nostalgia." In *Rhetorics of Self-Making*, ed. Debbora Battaglia, pp. 77–96. Berkeley: University of California Press.

Berman, Marshall, 1982 *All That is Solid Melts Into Air*. New York: Simon and Schuster.

Besnier, Niko, 1996 "Authority and Egalitarianism." In *Leadership and Change in the Western Pacific*, ed. Richard Feinberg and Karen Watson-Gegeo, pp. 93–128. London: Athlone Press.

Bottomore, T. B., 1964 *Elites and Society*. New York: Basic Books.

Bourdieu, Pierre, 1977 *Outline of a Theory of Practice*. Cambridge: Cambridge University Press.

Bradford, Phillips Verner and Harvey Blume, 1992 *Ota Benga*. New York: St. Martin's Press.

Brewer, John, 1985 "Commercialization and Politics." In *The Birth of a Consumer Society*, ed. Neil McKendrick, John Brewer and J. H. Plumb, pp. 195–262. Bloomington: Indiana University Press.

Brian, Roger, 1996 "For Mum." *National*, Port Moresby, 10 May, p. 30.

Burke, Peter, 1978 *Popular Culture in Early Modern Europe*. London: Temple Smith.

Burris, Val, 1986 "The Discovery of the New Middle Class." *Theory and Society*, 15: 317–49.

1987 "The Neo-Marxist Synthesis of Marx and Weber on Class." In *The Marx–Weber Debate*, ed. Norbert Wiley, pp. 67–90. Newbury Park, NJ: Sage Publications.

Carrier, James, 1995 *Gifts and Commodities*. London: Routledge.

Carrier, James and Achsah Carrier, 1989 *Wage, Trade and Exchange in Melanesia*. Berkeley: University of California Press.

Charles, Jeffrey, 1993 *Service Clubs in American Society*. Urbana: University of Illinois Press.

Clifford, James, 1988 "Histories of the Tribal and the Modern." In *The Predicament of Culture*, ed. James Clifford, pp. 189–214. Cambridge, MA: Harvard University Press.

Cole, Rodney, ed., 1993 *Pacific 2010: Challenging the Future*. Canberra: National Centre for Development Studies.

Connell, John and John P. Lea, 1993 *Pacific 2010: Planning the Future*. Canberra: National Centre for Development Studies.

Connolly, Bob and Robin Anderson, 1984 *First Contact*. Video recording, Arundel Productions, New York Filmmakers Library.

1987 *First Contact*. New York: Viking Penguin.

Conyers, Diana, 1979 *The Provincial Government Debate*. Boroko, Papua New Guinea: Institute of Applied Social and Economic Research.

Curtain, Richard, 1984 "Ethnicity and Class in the Third World." In *Social Stratification in Papua New Guinea*, ed. R. J. May, pp. 119–32. Canberra: Australian National University Press.

Earle, Peter, 1989 *The Making of the English Middle Class*. Berkeley: University of California Press.

Errington, Frederick, 1987 "The Rock Creek Auction: Contradiction Between Competition and Community in Rural Montana." *Ethnology*, 26: 297–311.

Errington, Frederick and Deborah Gewertz, 1987 *Cultural Alternatives and a Feminist Anthropology*. Cambridge: Cambridge University Press.

1988 "Exemplars and the Reproduction of Everyday Life." *Dialectical Anthropology*, 13: 31–43.

1995 *Articulating Change in the "Last Unknown"*. Boulder, CO: Westview Press.

1996 "The Individuation of Tradition in a Papua New Guinea Modernity." *American Anthropologist*, 98: 114–26.

1997 "The Rotary Club of Wewak: The Middle Class in Papua New Guinea." *Journal of the Royal Anthropological Institute*, 3: 333–53.

Feinberg, Richard, 1978 "Rank and Authority on Anuta Island." In

Adaptation and Symbolism: Essays on Social Organization, ed. Karen Watson-Gegeo and S. Lee Seaton, pp. 1–32. Honolulu: University of Hawaii Press.

Filer, Colin, 1990 "The Bougainville Rebellion, the Mining Industry and the Process of Disintegration in Papua New Guinea." In *The Bougainville Crisis*, ed. R. J. May and Matthew Spriggs, pp. 73–112. Bathurst, Australia: Crawford House Press.

Fito, Gabriel, 1997 "East Sepik People Denied Services." *National*, 8 September, p. 2.

Fitzpatrick, Peter, 1980 *Law and State in Papua New Guinea*. London: Academic Press.

Foster, Robert, 1992 "Take Care of Public Telephones." *Public Culture*, 4: 31–45.

1995 "Print Advertisements and Nation Making in Metropolitan Papua New Guinea." In *Nation Making*, ed. Robert Foster, pp. 151–81. Ann Arbor: University of Michigan Press.

1997 "Commercial Mass Media in Papua New Guinea." *Visual Anthropology Review*, 12: 1–17.

1998 "Your Money, Our Money, the Government's Money." In *Border Fetishisms: Material Objects in Unstable Places*, pp. 60–90. London: Routledge.

Friedman, Jonathan, 1992 "Narcissism, Roots and Postmodernity: The Constitution of Selfhood in the Global Crisis." In *Modernity and Identity*, ed. Scott Lash and Jonathan Friedman, pp. 331–66. Oxford: Basil Blackwell.

Fry, Greg, 1997 "Framing the Islands." *Contemporary Pacific*, 9: 305–44.

Garcia-Canclini, Nestor, 1993 *Transforming Modernity: Popular Culture in Mexico*. Austin: University of Texas Press.

Gewertz, Deborah, 1983 *Sepik River Societies: A Historical Ethnography of the Chambri and their Neighbors*. New Haven: Yale University Press.

Gewertz, Deborah and Frederick Errington, 1991a *Twisted Histories, Altered Contexts: Representing the Chambri in a World System*. Cambridge: Cambridge University Press.

1991b "We Think, Therefore They Are?" *Anthropological Quarterly*, 64: 80–91.

1995 "Dueling Currencies in East New Britain: The Construction of Shell Money as National Cultural Property." In *Occidentalism*, ed. James Carrier, pp. 161–91. Oxford: Oxford University Press.

1996 "On PepsiCo and Piety in a Papua New Guinea 'Modernity.'" *American Ethnologist*, 23: 476–93.

1997 "Why We Go Back to Papua New Guinea." *Anthropological Quarterly*, 70: 127–36.

1998 "Sleights of Hand and the Construction of Desire in a Papua New Guinea Modernity." *Contemporary Pacific*, 10: 345–68.

Giddens, Anthony, 1973 *The Class Structure of the Advanced Societies.* London: Hutchinson University Library.

1991 *Modernity and Self-Identity.* Cambridge: Polity Press.

Godelier, Maurice, 1977 *Perspectives in Marxist Anthropology.* Cambridge: Cambridge University Press.

Gooden, Bruce, 1997 "We've Lowered Your Rate." Advertisement, First Card.

Goody, Jack, 1982 *Cooking, Cuisine and Class.* Cambridge: Cambridge University Press.

Harrison, Simon, 1982 "Ritual Hierarchy and Secular Equality in a Sepik River Village." *American Ethnologist*, 12: 413–26.

Harvey, David, 1989 *The Condition of Post-Modernity.* Oxford: Basil Blackwell.

Hau'ofa, Epeli, 1987 "The New South Pacific Society: Integration and Independence." In *Class and Culture in the South Pacific*, ed. Antony Hooper, *et al.*, pp. 1–15. Suva and Auckland: Centre for Pacific Studies.

Hayes, Geoffrey, 1994 "PNG's Population Prospects: Is Disaster Looming?" *Times of Papua New Guinea*, 14 July.

1995 "Review of Pacific 2010: Challenging the Future." *Contemporary Pacific*, 7: 191–94.

Hobsbawm, Eric and Terence Ranger, 1983 *The Invention of Tradition.* Cambridge: Cambridge University Press.

Hochschild, Arlie, 1997 *The Time Bind.* New York: Henry Holt.

Hooper, Antony, n.d. "Class in the South Pacific." Unpublished manuscript.

Hooper, Anthony and Judith Huntsman, 1990 "History and the Representation of Polynesian Societies." In *Culture and History in the Pacific*, ed. Jukka Siikala, pp. 9–24. Helsinki: Finnish Anthropological Society.

Hopkins, Adan and Gaby McPhedren, 1985 *Law and Order.* London: MacDonald.

Howard, Alan, 1996 "Money, Sovereignty and Moral Authority on Rotuma." In *Leadership and Change in the Western Pacific*, ed. Richard Feinberg and Karen Watson-Gegeo, pp. 205–38. London: Athlone.

Howard, Alan and Jan Rensel, 1994 "Rotuma in the 1990s: From Hinterland to Neighbourhood." *Journal of the Polynesian Society*, 103: 227–54.

Hunt, Margaret, 1996 *The Middling Sort: Commerce, Gender and the Family in England, 1680–1780.* Berkeley: University of California Press.

Independent, 1996 "Birthday Greeting." Port Moresby, 17 May, p. 26.

Injia, Salamo, 1997 "In the Matter of an Application Under Section 57 of the Constitution." Papua New Guinea National Court, M.P. No. 289 of 1996.

Jacob, Margaret, 1981 *The Radical Enlightenment: Pantheists, Freemasons and Republicans.* London: Allen and Unwin.

Jacobsen, Michael, 1995 "Vanishing Nations and the Infiltration of Nationalism." In *Nation Making*, ed. Robert Foster, pp. 227–49. Ann Arbor: University of Michigan Press.

Jameson, Fredric, 1991 *Postmodernism or the Cultural Logic of Late Capitalism*. London: Verso.

Johnson, Pat, 1993 "Education and the 'New' Inequality in Papua New Guinea." *Anthropology and Education Quarterly*, 24: 183–203.

Jolly, Margaret and Mark Mosko, eds., 1994 "Transformations of Hierarchy." *History and Anthropology*, 7.

Josephides, Lisette, 1985 *The Production of Inequality*. London: Tavistock.

Joyce, Patrick, 1995 "A People and a Class." In *Class*, ed. Patrick Joyce, pp. 161–67. Oxford: Oxford University Press.

Kantor, Rosabeth Moss, 1989 *When Giants Learn to Dance*. New York: Simon and Schuster.

Kearney, Michael, 1995 "The Local and the Global." *Annual Review of Anthropology*, 24: 547–65.

Keesing, Roger, 1976 *Cultural Anthropology*. New York: Holt, Rinehart and Winston.

1996 "Class, Culture, Custom." In *Melanesian Modernities*, ed. Jonathan Friedman and James Carrier, pp. 162–82. Lund, Sweden: Lund University Press.

Kildea, Gary and Jerry Leach, 1975 *Trobriand Cricket*. Ronin Films, Campbell, ACT, Australia.

Klein, Bradley, 1997 *Rough Meditations*. Chelsey, MI: Sleeping Bear Press.

Kuble, Ennio, 1997 "Population Growing Faster Than Economy." *National*, 14 July, p. 1.

Kulick, Donald, 1992 *Language Shift and Cultural Reproduction*. Cambridge: Cambridge University Press.

Lash, Scott and Jonathan Friedman, eds., 1992 *Modernity and Identity*. Oxford: Basil Blackwell.

Lawrence, Peter, 1964 *Road Belong Cargo*. Manchester: Manchester University Press.

Lekachman, Robert, 1977 "Capitalism." In *Harper Dictionary of Modern Thought*, ed. Alan Bullock, Oliver Stallybrass and Stephen Trombley, pp. 106. New York: Harper and Row.

Levine, Harold and Marilyn Levine, 1979 *Urbanisation in Papua New Guinea*. Cambridge: Cambridge University Press.

Lindstrom, Lamont, 1993 *Cargo Cult*. Honolulu: University of Hawaii Press.

Lipset, Seymour Martin, 1985 "Social Stratification and Social Class Analysis." In *Consensus and Conflict: Essays in Political Sociology*, ed. S. M. Lipset, pp. 45–79. New Brunswick, NJ: Transaction Books.

Lukács, Georg, 1971 *History and Class Consciousness*. Cambridge, MA: MIT Press.

Lutkehaus, Nancy, 1996 "'Identity Crisis': Changing Images of Chieftainship in Manam Society." In *Leadership and Change in the Western Pacific*, ed. Feinberg, Richard and Karen Watson-Gegeo, pp. 343–75. London: Athlone.

Mai, Evoa Mora, 1996 "Blame the Crime on Wide Rich–Poor Gap." *National*, 13 November, p. 1.

Marcus, George, ed., 1983 *Elites*. Albuquerque: University of New Mexico Press.

Marcus, John Ronduma, 1997 "Axe These Costly Special Days." *National*, 11 September, p. 7.

Marden, Charles, 1935 *Rotary and its Brothers*. Princeton: Princeton University Press.

Martin, Emily, 1994 *Flexible Bodies*. Boston: Beacon Press.

May, R. J., 1984 "Class, Ethnicity, Regionalism and Political Parties." In *Social Stratification in Papua New Guinea*, ed. R. J. May, pp. 174–90. Canberra: Australian National University Press.

McKendrick, Neil, John Brewer and J. H. Plumb, 1985 *The Birth of a Consumer Society*. Bloomington: Indiana University Press.

Mead, Margaret, 1970 *The Mountain Arapesh: Arts and Supernaturalism*. Garden City, NY: Natural History Press.

Miller, Daniel, 1994 *Modernity: An Ethnographic Approach*. Oxford: Berg.

1995 *Acknowledging Consumption*. New York: Routledge.

1997 *Capitalism: An Ethnographic Approach*. Oxford: Berg.

Millett, John, 1993 "The Unemployment Problem." In *Seminar on Employment, Agriculture and Industrialisation*, ed. John Millett, pp. 9–32. Port Moresby: Institute of National Affairs and the National Research Institute.

Miria, Clement, 1996 "Crime Threat to Investment." *National*, 8 May, pp. 1–2.

Modjeska, Nicholas, 1982 "Production and Inequality." In *Inequality in New Guinea Highlands Societies*, ed. Andrew Strathern, pp. 50–108. Cambridge: Cambridge University Press.

1995 "Rethinking Women's Exploitation: The Duna Case and the Material Basis of Big Man Systems." In *Papuan Borderlands*, ed. Aletta Biersack, pp. 265–85. Ann Arbor: University of Michigan Press.

Moore, Clive, 1990 "Workers in Colonial Papua New Guinea." In *Labour in the South Pacific*, ed. Clive Moore, Jacqueline Leckie and Doug Munro, pp. 30–46. Townsville Queensland: James Cook University Press.

Mydans, Seth, 1997a "In Lush Tropics, a Flowering of Murderous Gangs." *New York Times*, 1 May, p. A4.

1997b "As Election Nears, More Than Politics Divides." *New York Times*, 27 April, A4.

1997c "When the Bartered Bride Opts Out of the Bargain." *New York Times*, 6 May, p. A4.

1997d "Where All is Babel, They Spread the Good Word." *New York Times*, 20 May, p. A4.

1997e "Street Crime Plagues Papua New Guinea." *New York Times*, 22 June, Section 5, p. 3.

Narakobi, Bernard, 1980 *The Melanesian Way.* Boroko, Papua New Guinea and Suva, Fiji: Institute of Papua New Guinea Studies and Institute of Pacific Studies.

National, 1996a "Families Caught in a Vicious Wage Trap." Editorial, 9 December, p. 7.

1996 "Condolence Message." Port Moresby, 19 May, p. 30.

Nicholl, David Shelley, 1984 *The Golden Wheel.* Estover, Plymouth: MacDonald and Evans.

O'Faircheallaigh, Ciaran, 1992 "The Local Politics of Resource Development in the South Pacific: Towards a General Framework of Analysis." In *Resources, Development and Politics in the Pacific Islands*, ed. Stephen Hennigham and R. J. May, with Lulu Turner, pp. 258–89. Bathurst, Australia: Crawford House Press.

O'Hanlon, Michael, 1993 *Paradise.* London: British Museum.

Obeyesekere, Gananath, 1992 *The Apotheosis of Captain Cook.* Princeton: Princeton University Press.

Ogan, Eugene, n.d.a. "Culture, Class and the Modern Pacific Island State." Unpublished manuscript.

n.d.b "Class and Other Inequalities in Contemporary Papua New Guinea." Unpublished manuscript.

Ogan, Eugene and Terence Wesley-Smith, 1992 "Papua New Guinea: Changing Relations of Production." In *Social Change in the Pacific Islands*, ed. A. B. Robillard, pp. 35–64. New York: Kegan Paul International.

Ortner, Sherry, 1984 "Theory in Anthropology Since the Sixties." *Comparative Studies in Society and History*, 26: 126–66.

1991 "Reading America: Preliminary Notes on Class and Culture." In *Recapturing Anthropology: Working in the Present*, ed. Richard Fox, pp. 163–89. Santa Fe, NM: School of American Research.

Ossowski, Stanislaw, 1963 *Class Structure in the Social Consciousness.* London: Routledge and Kegan Paul.

Palme, Robert, 1996a "Girl Sold in Death Compo." *Post-Courier*, 3–5 May, p. 1.

1996b "Judge Looks Into Girl Compo Case." *Post-Courier*, 9 May, pp. 1–2.

Parkin, Frank, 1979 *Marxism and Class Theory: A Bourgeois Critique.* New York: Columbia University Press.

Parry, Jonathan, 1989 "On the Moral Perils of Exchange." In *Money and the Morality of Exchange*, ed. Jonathan Parry and Maurice Bloch, pp. 64–93. Cambridge: Cambridge University Press.

"Participation at 1996 Jayapura Expo," 1996. Unpublished manuscript. Wemak, PNG: Office of Commerce and Industry.

PEC Information Paper, 8 November, 1995 "Formation of Sepik Women in Trade Association." Wewak, PNG: Office of Commerce and Industry.

Philibert, Jean-Marc, 1986 "The Politics of Tradition: Toward a Generic Culture in Vanuatu." *Mankind*, 16: 1–12.

Robie, David, 1995 "Ownership and Control in the Pacific." In *Nius Bilong Pacific: Mass Media in the Pacific*, ed. David Robie, pp. 5–15. Port Moresby: University of Papua New Guinea Press.

Romaine, Suzanne, 1995 "Birds of a Different Feather." *Contemporary Pacific*, 7: 81–123.

Runciman, W. G., 1969 "The Three Dimensions of Social Inequality." In *Social Inequality: Selected Readings*, ed. Andre Beteille, pp. 47–63. Harmondsworth: Penguin.

Ryan, Dawn, 1978 "Cliques, Factions, and Leadership Among the Toaripi of Papua." In *Adaptation and Symbolism: Essays on Social Organization*, ed. Karen Ann Watson-Gegeo and S. Lee Seaton, pp. 33–48. Honolulu: University of Hawaii Press.

Rydell, Robert, 1984 *All the World's a Fair: Visions of Empire at American International Expositions, 1876–1916*. Chicago: University of Chicago Press.

Sandomir, Richard, 1997 "Tiger Woods Signs Pact With American Express." *New York Times*, 20 May, D1 and D8.

Schama, Simon, 1987 *The Embarrassment of Riches*. New York: Knopf.

Schlesinger, Arthur, 1946 *Learning How to Behave: A Historical Study of American Etiquette Books*. New York: MacMillan Company.

Scott, Joan, 1995 "Language, Gender and Working-Class History." In *Class*, ed. Patrick Joyce, pp. 154–61. Oxford: Oxford University Press.

Sklair, Leslie, 1991 *Sociology of the Global System*. Baltimore: Johns Hopkins University Press.

Smith, Charles, 1990 *The Social Construction of Value*. Berkeley: University of California Press.

Standish, William, 1979 *Provincial Government in Papua New Guinea*. Boroko, PNG: Institute of Applied Social and Economic Research.

Stedman Jones, Gareth, 1995 "Class, 'Experience', and Politics." In *Class*, ed. Patrick Joyce, pp. 150–54. Oxford: Oxford University Press.

Strathern, Andrew, 1982 "Two Waves of African Models in the New Guinea Highlands." In *Inequality in New Guinea Highlands Societies*, ed. Andrew Strathern, pp. 137–57. Cambridge: Cambridge University Press.

1984 *A Line of Power*. London: Tavistock.

Strathern, Marilyn, 1975 "No Money on Our Skins." Port Moresby: New Guinea Research Bulletin, 61.

1985 "John Locke's Servant and the Hausboi from Hagen." *Critical Philosophy*, 2: 21–48.

1988 *The Gender of the Gift*. Berkeley: University of California Press

1992 "The Decomposition of an Event." *Cultural Anthropology*, 7: 244–54.

Taka, Daniel, 1996 "Crime Only a Symptom of a Problem." *Post-Courier*, 17 May, p. 10.

Tannos, Jonathan, 1996 "No. 2 PM Gets Chiefly Title at Home." *Post-Courier*, Friday–Sunday, 10–12 May, p. 1.

Taylor, Charles, 1989 *Sources of the Self*. Cambridge, MA: Harvard University Press.

Thomas, Nicholas, 1991 *Entangled Objects*. Cambridge, MA: Harvard University Press.

1994 *Colonialism's Culture*. Princeton: Princeton University Press.

Thompson, E. P., 1964 *The Making of the English Working Class*. New York: Pantheon.

1978 "Eighteenth-Century English Society: Class Struggle Without Class?" *Social History*, 3: 133–65.

Thompson, Herb and Scott MacWilliam, 1992 "From Acquisition to Accumulation." In *The Political Economy of Papua New Guinea*, ed. Herb Thompson and Scott MacWilliam, pp. 85–119. Manila: *Journal of Contemporary Asia*.

Thompson, Patricia, 1989 *Stolen Moments: A Story of Love and Intrigue in Contemporary Mount Hagen*. Tilkil Kaun Productions, Port Moresby.

Thurow, Lester, 1997 "What's Ahead for Working Men and Women?" *New York Times*, 31 August, p. E9.

Tobia, Brian, 1996 "Beat Crime With Jobs – Business." *Post-Courier*, 16 May, p. 1–2.

Tobin, Jeff, 1992 *Re-Made in Japan*. New Haven: Yale University Press.

Torgovnik, Marianna, 1990 *Gone Primitive*. Chicago: University of Chicago Press.

Turner, Mark, 1984 *Problems of Social Class Analysis in Papua New Guinea*. In Social Stratification in Papua New Guinea, ed. R. J. May, pp. 55–62. Canberra: Australian National University Press.

1990 *Papua New Guinea: The Challenge of Independence*. Harmondsworth: Penguin.

University of Chicago Social Science Survey Committee, 1934 *Rotary? A University Group Looks at the Rotary Club of Chicago*. Chicago: University of Chicago Press.

Updike, John, 1996 *Golf Dreams*. New York: Knopf.

Wacquant, Loic J. D., 1991 "Making Class: The Middle Class(es) in Social Theory and Social Structure." In *Bringing Class Back In*, ed. Scott G. McNail, Rhonda F. Levine and Rick Fantasia, pp. 39–64. Boulder, CO: Westview Press.

Weber, Max, 1956 *The Protestant Ethic and the Spirit of Capitalism*. New York: Scribner's Sons.

1968 "The Distribution of Power Within the Political Community: Class, Status, Party." In *Economy and Society*, ed. Guenther Roth and Claus Wittich, pp. 926–40. New York: Bedminster Press.

What is Wealth? n.d. Reserve Bank of Australia.

White, Geoffrey and Lamont Lindstrom, eds., 1998 *Chiefs Today*. Honolulu: University of Hawaii Press.

Wiley, Norbert, 1987 "Introduction." In *The Marx–Weber Debate*, ed. Norbert Wiley, pp. 7–27. Newbury Park, NJ: Sage Publications.

Wolfers, Edward P., 1992 "Politics, Development and Resources: Reflections on Constructs, Conflicts and Consultants." In *Resources, Development and Politics in the Pacific Islands*, ed. Stephen Henningham and R. J. May, with Lulu Turner, pp. 238–57. Bathurst, Australia: Crawford House Press.

Yombon, Phil, 1997 "Unequal Challenge." *National*, 30 May, p. 2.

Your Money, n.d. Reserve Bank of Australia.

Index